GETTING TO
'   US   '

Discover the Ability to Lead Your
Team to Any Result You Desire

JOE CURCILLO

THOUGHT EMPORIUM
LTD

Getting To 'US'
Discover the Ability to Lead Your Team to Any Result You Desire
by Joe Curcillo

For information, contact:

THOUGHT EMPORIUM LTD

Thought Emporium, Ltd.
3964 Lexington Street
Harrisburg, PA 17109
www.ThoughtEmporium.com

ISBN: 978-0-692-10294-7

LCCN: 2018904252

Printed in the United States of America

To my daughters, Olivia and Kaela.
… my favorite millennials.

CONTENTS

PART I

FIND THE RIGHT FUEL TO INSPIRE ACTION

CHAPTER 1

The Problem with Persuasion

"There could have been no two hearts so open,
no tastes so similar, no feelings so in unison."
Jane Austen

In July 2017, I arrived at a well-known Orlando resort for a conference and stepped right into a hive of construction. Although I passed a number of bellmen and hotel employees, I was not directed through the construction area, nor was I greeted with any hellos or smiles.

When I finally found the lengthy check-in line, the other guests were quick to let me know that it wasn't moving at all. As one woman left the reception desk, she looked back and said, "Good luck getting a room. Nothing seems to be ready!"

After about twenty minutes, it was finally my turn, and as I approached the desk, I glanced at the clerk's name badge. It read: "My name is Ed. My passion is hiking."

His perfect skin and well-groomed hair were overpowered by his perfect plastic smile. "Ed the Boy Scout," I thought.

"I guess I picked a busy time," I said, returning his smile.

"Yes," he replied, looking even more strained. "And none of the rooms are ready."

He checked me in and said that they would call when I could get my room. He directed me to the bell desk, where I could deposit my luggage—alongside everyone else's. José, whose "passion is motorcycles," spoke through a tight smile advising me to leave my bags, and adding, "We would be happy to bring them to your room when you get one." He spoke politely, but his smile failed to mask the stress in his eyes. As he addressed me, he glanced back and forth at the growing mountain of bags at his booth.

Just thirty minutes into my arrival, and I was able to predict the level of service that I would be receiving over the next five days.

I went to the restaurant to have a drink while I waited for my room. A manager welcomed me, then stomped over to a waitress and snarled, "You have someone at Table Seven."

The shift in his body language and vocal tone was so drastic that it seemed like the manager had changed from Dr. Jekyll to Mr. Hyde during the fifteen-foot walk from my table to the waitress station.

When the waitress approached me, I instantly realized that her bubbly warm personality was the opposite of everyone else that I'd met at the hotel. I smiled and said, "I'll have a cup of coffee, so long as you don't have mood swings like your boss."

She laughed and said, "You look exhausted; you must've just flown in. How about a triple espresso?"

We got along just fine. I do not remember her name tag or her passion, I only remember her cheerful demeanor. She seemed out of place.

Neither Ed the desk clerk nor José the bellman were un-caring people. They just had defaulted to a robotic stance under a set of rules that left no room for them to be themselves. It was as if management thought that giving them a name tag that stated their personal passion would be sufficient motivation for them to demonstrate passion for their work.

They were all doing the best that they could under the circumstances. As my waitress delivered a second triple espresso, I admired her personal desire to be kind. She was the first employee I'd encountered whose words did not seem pre-programmed. Her ability to snap back from the manager's scolding and walk over to me and treat me with such warmth made her one of those employees that management could point to and say, "Look, if she can do it, so can you."

But that is not effective management. There are exceptions to every situation, and some people are just more capable of operating under adverse circumstances. She is an anomaly, and management tends to underestimate the personal effort that someone in her situation exerts to be cheerful and welcoming.

Despite their efforts, the individual demeanors of most of the staff indicated that whatever passion was printed on the name tag certainly didn't carry over to their jobs. They did not seem to have passion for anything having to do with their work.

I assume the passion listed on the name badge was intended to be a conversation starter, a way of personalizing the employee and opening them up to conversation with the guests. Sadly, someone who is just going through the motions and clearly doesn't feel good about what they're doing isn't someone with whom I'd want to share stories about hiking or motorcycles.

When I was at the front desk checking in, it seemed to me that Boy Scout Ed should have been empowered to offer an explanation beyond "rooms are not ready" or even add an amenity to make up for the delay. While each employee I encountered was polite, it was evident that they were working diligently to keep within a script that wasn't designed to account for the frustration of trying to serve guests under difficult circumstances. The staff had not been empowered to make guests feel welcome. When you are focused on following a script, you cannot focus on the people in front of you.

This is what you get when management dictates the rules without inspiring the team. The absence of the heart and soul in the staff's attempts to do their jobs efficiently and happily was not the result of a lack of effort on their part, but the result of management treating them like cogs in a wheel and ignoring the possibility that maybe they could be more. And yet my waitress was an exception. What made her different? I wondered...

As I sipped my espresso, I reflected upon an experience that I'd had in 1985, when I was in my late twenties. I was having dinner with a group of friends, including Ted, a doctor in his early forties with a blond 1970s pageboy hairstyle and wire-rimmed glasses. Ted's idea of casual wear was a diligently pressed Izod shirt and a pair of creased Jordache jeans. He had an odd habit of speaking to people without ever making eye contact.

As his eyes wandered around the restaurant, Ted complained to the table about the office staff at his practice; "When I have someone trained, the employee finds a new job, or falls from 'great employee' status to mediocrity."

He was mystified, but I knew the answer. He saw his staff as trainable rather than capable. He had provided his staff with a series of obligatory tasks to perform without giving them the ability to merge their own talents and passion into the big picture. They did patient intakes, they took vitals, or they drew blood. They were assigned individual task after individual task. It was monotonous. He never showed them the big picture, but instead taught them their individual duties with no understanding of the larger contribution they made.

As Dr. Ted monopolized the conversation, I tried to listen without rolling my eyes. I think we all wanted to yell, "Hey, Ted. Maybe the problem is you!" We glanced at each other and just listened until I interrupted by joking, "I'm sorry, I couldn't figure out if you were talking about people or puppies."

Ted stopped his rant, looked at me and said, "That's rude. Why did you say that?"

I smiled as someone else giggled and said, "You sound like you would be happier if you hired people who jumped through hoops and sat on command."

In the discussion that followed, it became more and more clear that, to him, the people he called his team were merely cogs in a machine. Fundamentally, he saw them as office equipment. It was obvious to me that his staff knew he did not care about them; he only cared about how he wanted things done.

At the time, I was a young attorney—not a consultant and trainer—but I knew he was the problem. Even in court,

I realized that if I treated people the way he treated his employees, my successes would be few.

With that story in mind, I took another sip of espresso and chuckled to myself. The staff of this hotel was office equipment. My waitress had risen above it. The rest of them had not.

I received a call that my room was ready. It was 5:45, nearly three hours after I'd stepped in line. No explanation or apology, just a call to pick up my key.

Throughout my stay, I kept noticing the absence of a relationship between the guests and the staff. Only two weeks earlier, while I was staying in a casino in Las Vegas, every single employee I encountered smiled and said, "Thank you for staying at the Mirage. If you need anything, please let me know." Whether the maid was carrying dirty laundry, or the maintenance man was fixing a broken bathtub faucet, it didn't matter. They made me feel like I belonged. There was no script. Each spoke as if from the heart.

At my current hotel in Orlando, the lack of the promised "magic" was palpable. Since I knew the destination hosts over sixty million visitors per year, and boasts its luxury status, I expected a much warmer feel during my stay.

On the second day, I met Barbara. Barbara's name tag read, "My passion is family." She was one of the two house-keepers responsible for cleaning the scores of rooms on my floor.

One morning, I placed a decent tip for Barbara on my bed, and I left the room to get a cup of "not hotel room" coffee. When I returned, Barbara greeted me with her head down and said, "I'm sorry, there was money on your bed. drop it?"

I looked at her in amazement. "It's your tip. Don't people in this hotel tip you?"

In an unexpected burst of honesty, she replied, "People don't feel good about this place because of the management, and they take it out on us. So, no, we don't get many tips."

I was struck by her candid and direct response. She told me they had fewer than 150 members on the entire house-keeping staff. Realizing that the hotel had approximately 1,500 rooms, I did some quick math. Assuming that only a percentage of those were actual housekeepers or maids, they were under a lot of pressure.

Barbara continued. "The bosses don't understand what is being asked of the employees. We don't have enough help. They count the rooms we clean, but they almost never check our work." The hotel measured performance based on the quantity of rooms cleaned, not the quality of the work.

After a few moments of discussion, Barbara asked why I was so interested in the housekeeping. I told her that in my observations as a traveler, the attitude of the staff was a good barometer of the overall hotel operations. If the staff was not happy, my experience at that property would not be happy. I said, "The housekeepers are the face of the hotel, the first face I see when I leave my room."

Barbara's face lit up. "I never thought of my job as making me the face of a hotel. I'm just a housekeeper."

I told her, "I only see the front desk staff when I check in. I see the bellmen when they bring me my luggage, and I see the doorman when I come and go. But if I am in the halls of the hotel, it's the housekeeping staff that I see most."

Barbara surveyed my organized and neat hotel room and said, "I wish more guests were like you, because people leave their rooms messy and in disarray, and because they get bad service in the restaurant or at the front desk, they take out every little complaint on us!"

Barbara's honesty was refreshing. But at the same time, I noticed an exhausted look in her eyes, which were heavy and slightly red. She told me she was ahead of schedule, and time wasn't a problem, but she kept looking under a towel on her cart at her phone. I felt that there was more to her demeanor than just being overworked. I asked Barbara why she looked so sad. She told me that her daughter was on vacation in Belize that week, and she was concerned because she had uncharacteristically failed to call for four days.

As Barbara left, I gave her an additional tip for her time. Glancing back to her nametag, I said, "I know that family is your passion. I'm sure you'll hear from your daughter soon. She's probably just having fun."

Barbara's comments confirmed the perennial truth of an old Italian adage: "The fish rots from the head." While the staff may be stressed out and overworked, the problem lies with management who either hasn't given them the infrastructure they need to do their jobs or hasn't found a way to influence them into infusing their work with passion.

Initially, both Doctor Ted and the restaurant manager could push their employees into action to do what needed to be done, but they would never be loyal or self-motivated. They simply jumped through the hoops without having even an inkling of a larger goal.

To their deficit, management focused on numbers and volume without influencing the staff to create an excellent experience for their guests. They didn't empower their people to do anything beyond repeating the management's rote commentary.

It's up to management to inspire a passion for work in the hearts of the staff. Instead, management reserved all their kindness and concern for their interactions with the guests. And none of that kindness seemed to flow in the direction of the employees. The employees were just pushing the cart uphill to avoid being labeled as part of the problem. Their efforts to please management had consumed any attitude of kindness or sincerity they could muster with the guests. As a result, their attempts to care seemed fake. They were disengaged at work because management was disengaged from them.

It was clear to me that Dr. Ted in 1985 and the restaurant manager in 2017 had made the same error. Both failed to recognize the humanity and the personal need of each staff member to feel valuable. Later that day at the resort, I returned to my room and found a case of water and multiple bags of coffee sitting on the counter. I had acknowledged Barbara's humanity, and she showered me with the only gifts that she had access to: water and coffee from her cart.

The following morning, as I prepared to check out of my room, Barbara ran down the hall and hugged me saying, "My daughter is okay. Thank you." And she went back to work.

As I wheeled my luggage down the hall, I heard Barbara and her partner shouting "Good Morning!" to all the guests as they passed. Feeling important in the big picture is empowering. Feeling good about your contribution to the big picture is contagious.

I thought back on my career as both a businessman and an attorney. As a courtroom litigator, my success or failure hinged on my ability to persuade. Whether I was dealing with a client, a judge, a jury, or other lawyers, it was my job to persuade people to do as I asked. But I also recognized that the true art of persuasion required people to feel good about taking the action I requested. If they did not feel good about taking one action I asked for, they would never allow me to persuade them again. They would second-guess everything I said. Even the worst druggie-snitch witness in court needed to see a personal benefit before he would testify.

Coercing people to take an action is at the base level of influence. It is always possible, yet never produces better than mediocre results.

Moving others to take *inspired* action is the cornerstone of effective management. It is the cornerstone of sales. It is the cornerstone of any action that you take when you want others to follow your lead. Persuasion, when done effectively, leads to inspired action—action that people take as a result of an internal motivation to move closer to *your* goal because it is closer to *their* goal.

But if you hope to get inspired action by ordering people around or offering short-term incentives such as bonuses and other tokens of recognition, you'll be disappointed every time. While it motivates in the short term, it's not sustainable. Each reward (which is basically a bribe) will be followed by a demand for an even bigger one. Bribes are not what inspires people to extraordinary action or excellence. Believe it or not, humans are more noble than that.

Persuasion, when done effectively, leads to inspired action—action that people take as a result of an internal motivation to move closer to your goal because it is closer to their goal.

When I was a teenager, I worked in a fast food restaurant. Every week, the manager offered a five-dollar bonus for the best employee on the grill. I was sixteen. I was excited by the challenge. Living at home, rent-free, a five-dollar bonus meant I could buy an extra movie ticket or a jumbo popcorn. Plus, I liked winning. I worked as hard as I could to move burgers and win the coveted "Best Grill Person Award." For the first three weeks, I won and got my five dollars. As the fourth week began, I thought about Carson, the man who had come in second place for the past three weeks. Carson was in his early thirties, living alone with bills to pay.

I felt bad knowing that by winning, I was making life harder for Carson. I slowed down so he could get the five dollars. Shortly after his second victory, the manager reprimanded me for not working as hard. I laughed and went back to work. I didn't care what the manager thought of me. Knowing I was helping Carson was worth way more than five dollars.

People do not become engaged simply because you place demands on them. People do not want to put their heart and soul into something if they feel that their heart and soul will not benefit from the journey you are asking them to share with you. Incentives are only incentives until they become the norm; then they become expectations.

But people will sacrifice for a cause they believe in.

It is the objective of every leader to move people to accomplish the leader's vision. You can make your business a cause that your employees feel passionate about, but if you treat them like dogs who will only perform for a treat or a pat on the head, you will never get the best out of them. Absent a sense of value and purpose, people will always seek and find the path of least resistance. Achieving a long-term vision requires universal collaboration with people on your team who share that vision and are inspired by it.

A 2017 Gallup poll revealed that a mere 15% of employees worldwide are engaged at work. In the US, 30% of workers are engaged. Gallup defines engaged employees as those who are involved in, enthusiastic about, and committed to their work and workplace.[1]

At work, the poll showed that 70% of workers are engaged in everything and anything other than the matters in which they should be engaged. Employees like to spend time texting,

---

[1] http://news.gallup.com/poll/180404/gallup-daily-employee-engagement.aspx

checking Facebook, making weekend plans, or simply talking about what they're going to do for lunch.

If 30% of the people in the workforce are engaged at work, let's look at the obvious: in terms of productivity, three disengaged people make up less than one engaged employee.

Disengaged employees can produce numbers. You can see how many rooms they clean, or how many guests they check in, but without appropriate persuasion they will be uninspired; they will not invest in the bigger vision, and this will reflect negatively across the board.

It was clear that the resort management was using aggressive oversight to keep the maids cleaning, the front desk staff on script, and the guests committed to keeping their reservations despite the delays. In the short term, management got what it wanted, because everyone complied. But there is a huge opportunity cost. Much like the staff, the guests were not happily engaged in our relationship with the hotel. And I, for one, am not likely to return. In the long run, it's issues like these that kill businesses.

I have heard people claim that the art of persuasion is dead. One CEO told me, "Nobody wants to be talked into anything." Another small business owner insisted, "People are skeptical of everything. They don't believe what you tell them, so you can't persuade them like you could in the past."

They are right; people do not want to be manipulated or forced to do anything. Culturally, the word "persuasion" has become synonymous with manipulation and trickery. People will resist if they feel that they are about to be manipulated.

Forcing people to act without providing them the ability to feel proud about what they are doing will force a state where they feel less proud of their own accomplishments, and their actions will become rote.

If you try to force a horse to drink from the water trough, you will be unsuccessful. The good news is that you can put salt in his oats and make him thirsty. In management, you can create a thirst for excellence. Providing your team with a clear unifying vision will allow them to make a meaningful contribution and to be proud of their role in it.

As you read through these pages you will discover how to persuade people to become part of a unified team with clearly defined roles, and ultimately cause them to embrace your vision as their own. The key to effective persuasion is to start with learning to influence, and bringing in others to join you, as you master *Getting to Us*.

CHAPTER 2

People Want What They Want

"For success, like happiness, cannot be pursued;
it must ensue, and it only does so as the unintended
side effect of one's personal dedication to a cause
greater than oneself or as the by-product of one's
surrender to a person other than oneself."
Viktor E. Frankl, *Man's Search for Meaning*

The search for meaning is a quest that has existed since the beginning of time. While the focus of those seeking purpose has taken on many forms, the fundamental need for purpose remains unchanged. It is fashionable these days to blame management challenges on generational differences or the perceived need to manage each generation in its own special way, but these ideas are misguided, and pursuing them actually delays the solution and devours profit.

Throughout the years, there has been a common theme in management training that each generation brings with it a new problem to be solved. Whether the problem has revolved around baby boomers, the hippie generation, or millennials, there is always a newly labelled problem that management is trying to solve.

Let's make it perfectly clear that there is no "millennial problem." No generation is a problem.

Every generation gets trademarked with a label. These labels are superficial brandings that lump people into categories. When we take a management failure and label it as a generational problem, we are stereotyping an entire segment of society and generalizing the wants, needs, desires, and attitudes of millions of people with the illusion that these are all somehow predictable by the year of a person's birth. If you think that every millennial requires an ability to work from home, you are no more likely to be correct than you are to assume that every baby boomer wants to avoid the internet or that every Gen-Xer is independent, resourceful, and self-sufficient. These broad sweeping conclusions are the types of voodoo that keep Angela, the psychic advisor next door to my office, in the black. If a cold reading of a generation is what you desire, visit Angela; she is cheaper than a consultant, and probably more accurate.

The fact is, for every person who fits the generational stereotype in one particular area, you can find six more who don't. And listen, there's nothing wrong with playing the game of lumping people together and looking for traits that define a generation. Truth is, it's kind of fun. It's only a problem when we try to manage people by it.

Businesses today spend millions of dollars to explore the "issues" tied to employing people from various generations, and to teach their managers how to deal with them. A 2017 search on Google for the phrase "the millennial problem" yielded 3,470,000 results. The "generational problem" produced 15,300,000 results, so clearly enough people perceive a problem to have gone to the trouble to provide a lot of answers. And if you wonder how much money companies are spending to deal with it, a search for "consultants generational problem" yielded 385,000 hits, a clear sign that the repetition of the label "millennial problem" has perpetuated and fostered the growth of an entire industry devoted to training and educating us to deal with this mysterious generation. But let's get real: The mystery that an older generation feels when looking at a new one happens with each and every turn of the tide. One generation is born into the inventions and discoveries of all prior generations, and all prior inventions and discoveries become the birthright of the new generation. But none of this has anything to do with how to manage or to influence your team. When managers blame their inability to motivate their people on "the generational problem" and label an entire age group, it's beyond folly; it's debilitating.

Labels become self-fulfilling prophecies. If a baby boomer says that the entire millennial generation consists of people with a philosophy that they are entitled to receive in lieu of actually doing work, the boomer will be disinclined to trust them to get a job done, and thus, lose out on the millennial's natural talents and desire to succeed. If you are hesitant to assign tasks to people you have labeled, you will never have the opportunity to see them shine.

And it goes both ways. If millennials label the baby boomers as non-tech-savvy people with no vision for the future, they are overlooking the experience of the boomer who grew up in a tumultuous political time, and who happens to be of the generation that invented the technology at which many millennials are so adept. Thus, the millennial overlooks the individual boomers who possess vision and compatible skills. In the end, any label that you apply to a person, generational or otherwise, will often dictate the results that you get from that person, which is why I'm against it. In truth, if your interest is figuring out how to manage and motivate your teams, there is only one label that can be of any help at all— "human being."

In 2007, while serving as a juvenile law judge in Dauphin County, Pennsylvania, a minor came before me on serious charges that would have placed an adult in prison for a very long time. Ken was sixteen years old and could only remain in the juvenile system until he was 21. His crimes and attitude made me wish I could keep him locked away forever.

Every six months for the next five years he was brought before me and every time our discussions ended with him telling me that he planned to re-offend, and I sent him back to juvenile detention. When Ken was 20 1/2 years old, he came before me for his final six-month review hearing. I knew I would never see him again, and I knew that within six months he would be free. The hearing was brief and followed the same course as the ones that came before: He said he would re-offend. I said, "I hope that someday I meet you on the street and find out that you have become a good father and husband. If I do not meet you on the street, I will know that you were re-incarcerated as an adult. If that happens, our paths will never cross, and I will know that you failed." Then I sent him back to lockup.

Six years later, in 2013, my secretary told me that there was someone in my waiting room. "He says his name is Ken, and you will remember him."

As soon as I saw him I remembered his face. I ushered him into my conference room and tersely asked, "What can I do for you?"

He smiled and said, "I just wanted to thank you for all you did for me."

"What did I do?"

Ken explained that, through his years in the system, he felt he had been treated like an animal. Everyone told him what to do and locked him in cages. But every time he appeared in front of me, "You treated me like a human being. I may not have liked what you said to me, but you never lied or sugarcoated the truth. You always made sure I understood our conversation. Then you locked me back up."

I smiled and said, "You know, you didn't give me a choice."

He replied, "The last time I saw you, you gave me a choice of being a husband and father or a prisoner. Everyone else told me I would be a prisoner forever. I wanted you to know that I am getting married this weekend. You are the only person who ever gave me the option to believe in myself." He laughed as he continued, "You were a bit of a jerk about it, but I wouldn't have heard you otherwise, because I was a jerk too. Thank you."

I admit, I didn't consciously intend to give Ken a cause he could believe in, I just explained his options as I saw them. He chose the right one. He made the human choice. The noble choice.

If we drop stereotypes and labels and just focus on basic human nature, we can see that all human beings fundamentally want and need the same things—a roof over their heads, food in their bellies, and a sense of belonging to or contributing to a community or a cause. As an employer, if you want high performance, high engagement, and high retention, you must provide an environment where your employees have the opportunity to achieve all three.

Most jobs only provide the opportunity for employees to meet the first two: food and a place to live. Some drop even below *that* bar and fail to pay a living wage while using threats of reprisals to "motivate." This is not anyone I'm interested in working with, so I'm not going to spend a lot of time on all the reasons why a strategy of threats is ineffective. Suffice it to say, this behavior only causes resentment, poor retention, and passive-aggressive behaviors that work against the company's aims.

More common is employers who use financial rewards and incentives to motivate people into being high performers. Unfortunately, if the primary motivator is cash, even those who are paid well and have benefits that exceed the norm will never stop looking for higher incentives at your company or elsewhere. People will perform for financial reward, but financial reward does not buy loyalty. The singular incentive of financial gain in exchange for meeting a certain metric may produce for a while, but then workers likely will require more incentives to remain, or they will move on to the next opportunity leaving you with the loss of their talent and a position to fill.

High performance and high retention can only be gained when we include the third element: a sense of belonging or contribution to a community or cause. Loyalty is what we think of when we see people committed to a cause. In most situations, serving a higher cause will win out over financial gain.

If you read this and still have doubts, consider this: If financial gain were truly the key factor to motivating people, ask yourself why so many volunteer their time and give their money away to support causes that are important to them. People are motivated and inspired by a cause they can believe in, a cause that inspires them to make a noble and important contribution. If you want to motivate your employees for the long haul, without breaking the bank, make your business, project, or department their cause, and show them their integral role in it.

High performance and high retention can only be gained when we include the third element: a sense of belonging or contribution to a community or cause.

A sense of nobility and honor is what moves us to sacrifice our immediate personal wants for something greater. If you think it can only happen in the volunteer realm, that it could never happen at a "job," let's move over to the most maligned of all workers, the ones who tend to be viewed with the lowest expectations with regard to motivation or desire for high performance: government employees.

On September 12, 1962, President John F. Kennedy told the nation, "We choose to go to the Moon in this decade and do the other things, *not* because they are easy, *but because they are hard*; because *that goal* will serve to organize and measure the best of our energies and skills, because *that challenge* is one that we are willing to accept, one we are unwilling to postpone, and *one we intend to win*."

This challenge fueled a generation. It came at a time when the US was trailing the Soviet Union in space initiatives, and the Cold War was at its peak. Winning was everything. The challenge gave people purpose and meaning, and they embraced the goal with vigor. It created a unifying vision that allowed countless people to be in that moment as one. We all shared equally in the success even though only three men risked their lives. Neil Armstrong's leap was truly for all mankind. And, more importantly, we as a nation believed it.

On July 20, 1969, no one at the Manned Spaceflight Center (now the Lyndon B. Johnson Space Center), in Houston complained about the long hours, or pulled their manager off the control panel to squawk about overtime.

Stereotypes and labels had taken a backseat to the cause. The thousands of NASA workers, government employees all, monitored all systems and ensured the safety of the three astronauts, and the world watched one team dedicated to one dream put a man on the Moon.

During the landing, Buzz Aldrin reported some drifting of the craft. Mission Control warned them that there was only thirty seconds of fuel to complete the landing. The world held its breath until Neil Armstrong radioed the now famous words, "Houston, Tranquility Base here. The Eagle has landed."

As the world listened to Neil Armstrong's communication, we saw the video and photographs of the countless people working at their stations in Mission Control. We know that these were the people who worked diligently to keep the astronauts alive. What we did not see were the countless people in the shadows. Of the many people working behind the scenes, most are still unknown to the public today. Now, fifty years later, the diligent commitment of the real "hidden figures" in the space program has come into view. In the segregated division of Langley Research Center in Hampton Virginia, Katherine Goble, Mary Jackson, Dorothy Vaughan, and hundreds of other team members followed the mission with extraordinary pride. These black female mathematicians—who were not in the public eye until a book about them, *Hidden Figures*, was published in 2016—were the human computers who physically calculated the trajectory of the Apollo craft. Without these unsung heroes, the craft would never have made it to the Moon.

Additionally, there were thousands of other employees who bought into the vision and played a role in its success—from the maintenance workers who kept the air conditioning circulating through the many integrated NASA facilities to the staff in the press office who fielded phone calls. Everyone who supported the astronauts was vital. The unifying vision gave each person the ability to see how their role was necessary for the success of the mission and the safe return of the astronauts to Earth. If one single member of mission control and the support team failed to recognize and fulfill their contribution, the mission could have easily ended in tragedy.

The moral of the story: never overlook the importance of even the most minor member of your team.

People want to do the right thing, but they define the "right thing" by their own standards and ideals. People are not willing to follow blindly unless the leader and the cause provide something that is aligned with their sense of nobility and value.

Joining a cause, making donations, and putting in overtime without complaint all serve a human being's inherent need for a sense of self-worth. All people crave a sense that they are important, valuable, and good. Everyone wants to place their head on a pillow at night thinking that what they did that day made a difference. It's called self-esteem. And it's a core need of every human being.

To create a work environment that fills this need and thus elicits the best performance out of your team, you need to express a unifying vision and enroll them in it. If the vision matters to them, and they feel connected to it, people will do extra every time and give you more at every turn. More effort, more time, more productivity, more "engagement." If you empower them and give them room, they will choose self-sacrifice for the cause. People want to surrender to a higher purpose and answer the call to serve their higher nature. People are persuaded when they believe that a cause is authentic, of value to the greater good, and aligns with their personal values.

Imagine what would happen if your business and your goals were a *cause* that people would dedicate their lives to achieve.

The moral of the story: never overlook the importance of even the most minor member of your team.

CHAPTER 3

The Power of a Unifying Vision

*"Maybe the two different worlds we lived in weren't
so different. We saw the same sunset."*
S.E. Hinton, *The Outsiders*

The single most powerful unifying vision in US history was the Declaration of Independence. The founding fathers and those who fought for freedom under George Washington's command operated according to a unifying vision that was embraced by people from all walks of life and from every generation. Enlistment in the continental army began at age sixteen. The average age was between twenty and twenty-five, with some soldiers as young as eleven. Civilians in supportive roles—wives and other volunteers who assisted with nursing, cleaning, and cooking—accompanied the troops.

When the French joined with Washington to help defeat the British, they were led by Marquis de Lafayette. He was twenty-one years old when he arrived at Valley Forge. The legendary head of our navy, John Paul Jones, was twenty-eight. Betsy Ross was twenty-four. These historical figures, together with Aaron Burr, Thomas Jefferson, Dr. Benjamin

Rush and others were, by 2017 standards, millennials to the comparative baby boomers of a forty-eight-year-old George Washington, a seventy-year-old Ben Franklin, and seventy-eight-year-old Samuel Whittemore. Back then, all of these generations worked together and unified to "pledge to each other our lives, our fortunes, and our sacred honor." These noble closing words of the Declaration of Independence are the definition of unity.

In the year that followed, the British seized control of Philadelphia, the birthplace of the American unifying vision. This invasion might have infused fear into the colonists, but it only made their commitment stronger. They embraced the vision, and against all odds and reason, fought for it.

In December 1777, George Washington marched 12,000 troops twenty miles northwest from Philadelphia into Valley Forge. From this position, the army was close enough to remind the British of the colonists' commitment, yet far enough away to wait out the winter safe from attack.

The soldiers at Valley Forge were ill supplied, but they were not beaten. A visitor wrote in the *New Jersey Gazette* on Christmas Day 1777, that "It was natural to expect that they wished for more comfortable accommodations, after the hardships of a most severe campaign; but I could discover nothing like a sigh of discontent at their situation. On the contrary, my ears were agreeably struck every evening, in riding through the camp, with a variety of military and patriotic songs and every countenance I saw, wore the appearance of cheerfulness or satisfaction."

People need to belong to something
that gives them a purpose.

The troops endured the cold, disease, and starvation. Military records reveal that nearly 2,000 men perished during the encampment. Yet these troops remained loyal to the unifying vision under the most extreme circumstances.

People need to belong to something that gives them a purpose. In any circumstance, be it business or battle, finding a place and feeling valuable to an inspiring bigger picture is the ultimate incentive.

When you give people an opportunity to be part of a vision that is bigger than them, bigger than the company, bigger than *you*, it galvanizes them. Once unified in a common vision, they are more willing to put forth the effort to realize it. Suddenly their work transcends the daily grind and becomes something greater. It's about being of service. It's about pride. It's about changing the world.

First, there needs to be a big picture, one that can close any gap between people, that transcends all differences, all self-interest, and even personality clashes. For people to "buy" into a unifying vision, it must represent a nobler cause, and it must give every team member the ability to see their role in it. It cannot be transactional, or greed based, nor should it be personality driven. It must be a *unifying vision*.

Defining a Unifying Vision

"Tell me and I forget. Teach me and I remember.
Involve me and I learn."
Benjamin Franklin

When Mary Barra took over as the chair and CEO of General Motors in 2014, she became the first female CEO of a global automaker. In 2017, Barra topped *Fortune's* Most Powerful Women list.[2] Her vision for GM was "Driving GM to become the global industry leader in automotive technology and design, product quality and safety, customer experience, and business results. Positioning the company to define and lead the future of personal mobility."[3]

In this mission statement, Barra addressed a divided audience looking to her for guidance. The first part is directed at the shareholders. She's letting the investors know that it is her goal to make GM an industry leader. She needed them to know that she understood their concerns and invited them to trust her plan to turn the company around. But the last line, "Positioning the company to define and lead the future of personal mobility," is primarily for the workers. It is the "bigger than us" unifying vision of how GM will change the world. It is an invitation to every employee to become part of something great.

In the pre-Barra era, a statement like that was unimaginable. GM had a long history of digging in its heels and doing

[2] http://fortune.com/most-powerful-women/mary-barra-1/
[3] https://www.linkedin.com/in/mary-barra-29469712/

everything the same way that it always had. Innovation was not something that prior management had embraced.

In the early 2000s, General Motors was well recognized as being run with out-of-date practices and a "this is just the way we do it" attitude. It was failing. After a US government bailout, GM earned the nickname "Government Motors." Its reliance on bureaucracy from the government, and bureaucracy from within, had to have taken a toll on the raison d'etre of the 220,000 employees.

Barra's message clearly told everyone, "the old ways are gone, and a new dawn is ahead." She gave employees especially something to be proud of, and a goal to achieve. Her confidence, her vision to see GM rise from the ashes to become the auto industry's leader, was so bold that, from anyone else's perspective, it may have seemed too big. But, with her 37-year track record at GM and her reputation as a team manager, Barra assured the employees that every one of them was going to have a place in the company's resurgence. They would be part of General Motors' history-making comeback.

Ultimately, it is up to you, the leader, to keep the vision relevant in your own mind, so that you can stand before your people and keep it alive and relevant in theirs. If you lose sight of the unifying vision, you're toast. You will never convince anyone to follow you.

In the fall of 2017, I attended a business meeting with two friends: Mark and Jared, from Fargo, North Dakota. The meeting was held in the Philadelphia suburbs. Since I am a Philadelphia native, I offered to give them a tour. I knew I could teach them the proper way to order a cheesesteak, or make sure they got to the Italian market, but otherwise I didn't have a plan. I was a child the last time I thought about my city's tourist destinations.

We met for breakfast on Saturday morning. I told them that we were only ten minutes from a big grass field that people seemed to like to visit.

They asked me why people visited the field, and I replied, "Because it's Valley Forge."

Getting excited over the historical value of Valley Forge, they both smiled and said they would love to go there. My commentary on Valley Forge was not intended as sarcasm, but as someone who had seen it every day of my life, the place had lost meaning. Somewhere in the back of my mind I recalled the importance of the Valley Forge encampment, but I had come to a place in my life where I took this historic locale for granted.

I had visited Valley Forge countless times. I went there for a Boy Scout jamboree, on class trips, and in my twenties I used it as a place to park and do paperwork during law school. I remembered exactly where I parked, but I had forgotten about the story of what happened there and what Valley Forge represents.

Valley Forge had become commonplace to me. It wasn't a destination, nor was it a historical vision to behold. It was a park. And it was there every day of my life. I got used to it, just like you may not notice the color of your neighbor's mailbox, or the telephone pole in your front yard.

As I took Mark and Jared to see Valley Forge, I watched two grown men who had never seen it fill with awe and excitement. Through their eyes, I gained a new appreciation for this iconic place. I recaptured the feeling I'd had as a teenager when I led the Boy Scout jamboree. Memories of history lessons rushed back to me through their eyes. My sense of awe was renewed.

As I stood with them and read each historic marker and each monument, the magnitude of Valley Forge's place in American history rekindled itself in my thoughts. The inspiration came alive in my heart once again.

When you have a vision for your business, you must never let it grow stale. Although my brief conversation with Barbara the housekeeper inspired her to a higher level of work, I have no illusions that it was sustainable under the current management. Sadly, I predict her realization that she is the face of the hotel was short lived. Based on what I observed, management would not remind Barbara of her importance or reinforce her sense of value to a nobler cause beyond "clean 150 toilets today or else."

A big part of what gives a unifying vision its power is its inclusiveness. In many environments, leaders rely upon the top 20% of the team. By relying on a small group, you send a message to the other 80% that they are not important. This leads them to underperform. After all, you just showed them how insignificant they are. For a unifying vision to have the power to move everyone in your organization to a higher level of performance, it must include *everyone*, and everyone's role must be viewed and presented as essential.

Everyone involved in the process must be included and have a clear role in bringing the unifying vision to fruition. Even the lowliest employee must be reminded of their value. The quarterback is the player who gets the public accolades for a team's success, but a good coach knows to thank and reward each player and staff person that was part of the winning squad.

When you have a vision for your business, you must never let it grow stale.

CHAPTER 4

Prepare to Lead

*"A true artist is not one who is inspired,
but one who inspires others."*
Salvador Dali

Leadership is founded on an ability to get things done. It's how you do it that determines how hard you will have to work to get the result. When a manager wants to compel their employees to take action, the directive can be simple: "Do this or get fired." But the threat of being fired is not an inspiring motivator. Sure, you can get someone to do something they don't want to do, but you must factor in the cost of buyer's remorse. Even effective threats provide only a temporary fix. Inevitably, the employee will find a more palatable solution by seeking employment elsewhere or just becoming an apathetic cog.

An employee will take action to avoid a negative outcome, but they may resent you so much for threatening them that instead of doing what you want, they may plant seeds of rebellion and dissention. Maybe it will not be the next morning. Maybe not the next week. Maybe it will not happen for years, but eventually when you force someone to do something they don't want to do, they will end up hating you for it and hating their job.

The highest form of persuasion is the ability to influence someone to do something that they will embrace as their own. Beyond knowing it's in their best interest, your goal is to have them love the action as if it were their own idea. This is pure influence. It is leading someone to a decision that they feel in their heart and know in their mind is right. The person must know that they acted in their own best interest and/or the interest of the greater good. And they must credit you as the influencer who made that possible.

The true leader is not only a visionary, but a master influencer. Influence boils down to getting someone to enthusiastically embrace what you want them to do, even when they're not inclined to do it. Leadership is about getting everyone to move in a single direction toward a common goal. It is about moving from "you and me" and getting to "us".

When I talk about 'getting to us', I am not referring to negotiation. This is not about settling for anything. In negotiation, people strive for a win-win solution, but the general recommendation is that you go into the negotiation with the expectation that you will end up settling for something short of your desired outcome.

Influence, however, is not a matter of negotiation. Getting your staff to do what you want and be happy about it cannot fall into a gray area of what you'll settle for. You must have the power to influence them to achieve exactly what you require, or you will never see your vision brought to life. If your vision is negotiable, rethink your aspirations until it's firm.

*The highest form of persuasion is the ability
to influence someone to do something that
they will embrace as their own.*

The path that leads to your ultimate vision may vary depending upon the team you have assembled, but as your team works toward it, the vison's objectives should serve as the magnet that pulls everyone in a single direction. If people are drawn to your vision, they will instinctively follow you. It is the unifying vision that will point toward the only acceptable destination.

Once you make the determination that your vision is important to you, there is no best alternative for which you should settle. The best news of all is that if your team has adopted the vision and has unified with you in that vision, they will not want to settle for anything less either. It is that steadfast unwillingness to settle that will make your role as a leader much easier.

*Once you make the determination that your
vision is important to you, there is no best
alternative for which you should settle.*

Most of us are accustomed to settling for less than we envision. This is why I advise, as you prepare to lead, that you be willing to get out of your comfort zone. When you want someone to take action, there is that moment when you must be willing to wait for them to accept the challenge with the same commitment and vision that you possess. The fear of whether they will accept and carry out your mission or reject it cannot get in your way.

For those leaders who have trouble delegating and letting go, understand that once they have accepted and embraced your vision, you must be willing to trust their ability to carry it out, persevere through that fear, and maintain the courage to withstand challenges.

Communicate Your Respect and Trust

"A person's a person, no matter how small."
Dr. Seuss, *Horton Hears a Who!*

Back at General Motors, in 2016, CEO Mary Barra told a group of newly promoted mid-level executives, "Remember your whole career, how you've been talking about *them*? If only *they* would get it. If only *they* would work this out. Well, you are now *they*. If you don't like something, you have to talk to yourself."[4]

This message empowered the managers to take on problems and find solutions, but more importantly, it communicated that Barra saw their knowledge as valuable. Barra initiated an innovative management model that told people that the old

---

[4] https://www.fastcompany.com/3064064/mary-barra-is-remaking-gms-culture-and-the-company-itself

rules were being broken, and everyone could be a part of something new, something better. Barra inspired her mid-level managers to want to become leaders and solve problems rather than be cogs in the wheel. She led with a belief that if the behavior of top management changes, their teams will mirror that behavior.

Barra thrust upon her team accountability and responsibility that screamed, "I know you can do your job. You have my respect. Now, do the job." They held the keys to the company's success, the keys to their own contributions to the world of mobility. She energized her team by offering them decision-making ability that they never owned before.

The people you lead need to know that you respect their knowledge and ability. When you respect people, they will draw energy from your respect, and in return, bring life to the vision you share. Your ability to communicate will convey to them that you trust them with the job you have assigned.

Whether you are leading a small business of two employees or a company of 200,000, treat all people with respect, and let them know they are valued. By doing so, you will inspire their involvement in your vision.

As a leader, your primary job doesn't need to be beating your employees with a stick to keep them going. Instead, make your main focus holding the vision and reinforcing it. You must keep the unifying vision alive, or it will deteriorate. If you lose the vision, so goes your team. If you take your team's enrollment in the vision for granted, you will become the cause of your own failure. Unity requires that everyone be "all in" at all times.

In a unifying vision, everyone has a role to play. Never treat anyone as if they are disposable or easily replaced. There may be a hundred different individuals you need to motivate, but feeling vital and necessary to the whole is a common need that everyone possesses. Don't only focus on your top performers or those highest on the food chain. Always keep the entire field in view as you look toward those you influence. If people can see the vision, but don't understand where they belong in it, they are likely to become lost or distracted. No matter how lowly a person's job may seem, never lose sight of the fact that each one is a valuable, necessary member of the group.

Communication is always important. If you lead a larger company, individual dialogue with each team member may be impossible, but you can still address the team. People need to know they are an active essential part of the relationship. Their specific individual needs may vary, but the universal need to be important to the mission will invigorate all.

Everyone wants to be needed. No one wants to believe that they can be replaced. A manager may look at the people in the building's maintenance department and think, "Anyone can do that job." A CEO may look at junior management and think there are hundred more people just like them fighting for similar positions. A salesman may look at the customer and think there's always the next door. But, the moment the individual perceives that they are being seen in this way, your ability to influence will wane, because a sense of disrespect and an absence of value will fall upon your audience.

One way to get people engaged is to communicate that you are listening and that you value them. If you do this, you must genuinely care about the people with whom you are speaking. I had a boss who used to tell us, "My door is always open." But, once we went through that open door, we were reminded that we were not the boss as he shot down every solution we presented. He only *acted* as if he respected our opinions. Respect cannot be faked. People will see through you. False respect will set off their B.S. meter. When that occurs, all hope of generating respect will disappear.

Choose your words with care. When your communications convey your respect, your trust, and your belief that the recipients are important to you, people will listen. Imagine that you get two phone messages this afternoon.

Message one is,

"I would love to hear how your new project is going. We haven't caught up in a while. Want to know what's going on. Love to hear from you. Call; I'll buy drinks tonight."

Message two is,

"You have to hear what's been going on. I got promoted at work, my daughter is number one in her class, and my son got accepted to grad school. Gotta tell you about it. Call me; we'll have drinks tonight."

We both know which one you're going to call back first. Message one is all about you—the listener. The message is simple and clear. The caller cares about you and what you are doing. Your immediate reaction is to be more engaged with that person because they care. The second is much less enticing. Who wants to end a day hearing about how great someone *else* is doing? Let people know they are the focus of your vision. It is not about you. The vision comes first.

Nobody cares how wonderful you think you are. Everything *you* have accomplished and everything *you* have done is not going to make others connect and feel good about doing what you want them to do. Don't look for the stroke to your ego just yet. The ultimate trophy is more valuable than winning ribbons along the way. Respect your team with the same feeling of commitment with which you embrace your vision. Make the commitment contagious.

Every team member must understand where they fit in the big picture. People must be able to see that they are integral in the role that they have been assigned. Whether or not you ever speak to them, approach each and every one projecting the sense that you value them, that you see their importance to the vision. When people can see their vital role in the unifying vision, they will naturally assign more importance to it.

Respect your team with the same feeling of commitment with which you embrace your vision. Make the commitment contagious.

PART II

THE PATH TO INFLUENCE

*"Great things are done by a series of
small things brought together."*
Vincent Van Gogh

In Part II we'll break down the process of influence into three steps. First, we'll turn your sight inward to understand and manage *you*. We will explore how you see yourself and, perhaps more importantly, how you are perceived by those you wish to influence. Next, we'll discuss the art of creating roles, so that you can direct people towards the outcomes you desire. Last, we'll discuss the process of creating an inspiring vision that others will want to be a part of. It is within this framework that you will build a unified vision to move others to carry out your mission with enthusiasm.

Keep in mind that these steps are not meant to be taken in chronological order; they can be followed in whatever sequence the moment requires. The thought process behind effective influence requires that you pick and choose as the situation demands. The dynamics of a relationship may cause you to work in phases where you will repeat one or more steps over and over again. Therefore, feel free to move around within the steps to reach new heights.

CHAPTER 5

Know and Accept Yourself

"He who knows others is wise;
he who knows himself is enlightened."
Lao Tzu

A man wearing a ski mask goes to a local restaurant where he fakes a robbery and murders his paramour by shooting her in the back. The murderer is an actor who had been having a long-standing affair with his show's producer, but it fell apart when she negotiated his contract and skimmed a substantial portion of his fee as part of a blackmail scheme. The opening credits of the 1970s detective show *Columbo* roll. Fade to commercial.

Cut to Lieutenant Columbo, a short, disheveled man carrying a cigar and the squinty-eyed look of a man straining to figure something out. Wearing his trademark wrinkled trench coat, he arrives on the scene, knocking down lights and cameras. Apologizing for his clumsiness, he interrogates the suspect with seemingly innocuous and meaningless questions, which convince the target that he is harmless.

Finally, Colombo turns to leave. The suspect relaxes. That's when Columbo pauses, turns, and delivers his signature line: "One more question…"

As Columbo fumbles his way from scene to scene, the pesky, "one more question" ploys become more on point and more annoying to the suspect, until finally the killer catches on and says, "Why don't we just stop pretending that I am brilliant and you are stupid?"

Colombo smirks and continues through his inquiry right up to the moment he elicits a confession.

As interpreted by the perfectly cast Peter Falk, Columbo knows and accepts himself to the point where he can use everything he is to influence others, even his traits that may appear to be weaknesses. For example, he knew he tended to be disorganized, that he probably never met a barber or a dry cleaner, and that he didn't give a damn about neatness or appearances. Rather than hide those traits and seem more like a buttoned-down, clean-cut lawman, he embraced his frumpy nature and used it to his advantage to disarm suspects who would otherwise be on guard and see him as a threat. Likewise, for you to become your persuasive best, you must first turn your sights inward, so you can see and accept yourself for who you truly are.

You don't need others to like you to influence them, but you do need to know what they think of you so you can deal with it.

Since most of us have put a good deal of time and effort trying to become an "acceptable" person, and be perceived as such, the task of seeing your true nature can be easier said than done. This is where you can get a little help from your best friends. As you will soon find out, they know exactly who you are. You're not fooling anyone.

It's easy to hear the praise of others and mistakenly allow those accolades to form a self-review that says, "people love me because of what I do or because of who they think I am." While it may feel good for a moment, the downside is the accompanying fear that if they knew "the real you," the praise would stop, and you would be rejected or abandoned. This fear turns praise into pressure—pressure to maintain the image that you have worked so hard to project. The key to freedom is to become aware of the fact that people do see your faults, they just don't tell you about it. When you learn to embrace all of you, warts and all, you will not only gain more influence, you will unlock a tremendous amount of energy.

Know Who You Are. Everyone Else Does.

*"People who say they don't care what people think
are usually desperate to have people think
they don't care what people think."*
George Carlin

You might think, "I don't care what people think about me." Actually, you do. And you should. Not to seek their approval; that's a waste of time. You don't need others to like you to influence them, but you do need to know what they think of you so you can deal with it.

If you are going to influence people and lead them, how they see you has a major effect upon how they respond to you. You may be very focused and driven to accomplish your goals, but if the people you need on your side see your drive and focus as coming from a malignant self-interest, they may interpret your desires as a threat to their well-being and work against you. If they see you as aloof or clueless, they may interpret that as a lack of direction and use it to manipulate you or just leave and find a different opportunity. In either case, people will be reluctant to follow your lead.

To influence any person or group, they must trust in your ability to help them satisfy their needs, so wrap your head around the fact that you must be aware of what people think and figure out how others see you. I repeat: not so that you can seek their approval, but so you can direct their perception and focus to your advantage.

To influence any person or group, they must trust in your ability to help them satisfy their needs.

Being able to direct the perception of others has always been a fascination of mine. As a performing magician, I drew the audience's attention to where I wanted it by using physical objects; that is, I made people look at one hand while I did the trick with the other. I had perfected the art of making people watch what I wanted them to watch, and thus, see what I wanted them to see. But it was not until I began my legal career that I realized the secret to deliberately directing people's attention in order to persuade.

Here's a clue: You can't direct anyone else's focus until you stop focusing on what people think of you.

During my very first jury trial in November 1985, I prosecuted a man for stealing a motorcycle. My main witness to the crime was a convicted criminal, so his credibility was sketchy at best. I had tried a number of mock trials in law school and had earned high marks, but this was my first trial where real-life stakes were involved. I was nervous about having all eyes on me, and concerned about what the judge, jury, and other lawyers might think of my performance. Mostly, I was obsessed with whether or not I looked competent.

When I made my closing argument, I asked the jury to convict, and returned to my seat at counsel table. I was so nervous that sweat rolled down my calves, but I was stoic and felt certain that I had looked competent.

The verdict came back. "Not guilty." I had lost.

That evening, as I left the courthouse, the jury foreperson stopped me. "Was that your first trial?" she asked.

"Yes, it…"

"I thought so," she interrupted. "I told them that was the reason you looked so distracted and nervous."

I shook my head and blurted, "What do you mean?"

She smiled, "The other jurors, they thought you were lying because you were sweating profusely and kept looking at the judge. They thought something was wrong."

I said goodnight and thanked her. I returned to my office, deflated. My mind raced. Her words played over and over in a loop. *"They thought you were lying."*

I knew it was true. I had been so focused on what the judge thought of me that my sideways glances must have made me appear shifty. Although I believed my presentation to be true, my behavior projected discomfort. The effort I expended to look competent for the judge was interpreted by the jury as deceit. I was concerned I would do something wrong or, more accurately, I was worried I would look bad. No wonder they had come back with "not guilty." I had become a distraction and undermined my own arguments.

Now what? I thought. *My dream has always been to be a trial lawyer, and I look like a liar in court.*

When I returned home that night, I sat in my living room and reminded myself of everything that I had done right. In review, I saw that I had done everything correctly except for this: Instead of focusing on my case and the jury, I focused on myself and what the judge thought of my performance. My case had been destroyed by my own need for approval.

In the several weeks that passed before my next trial, I reminded myself, "Stop seeking approval. Stop thinking about yourself. It's twelve jurors and you. No one else in the courtroom matters. You have this."

I won my very next case.

What I found astonishing was that being comfortable in my own skin required no work. I was just me. I did not try to be who I thought the judge wanted me to be. I stopped trying to impress the judge and focused on communicating effectively to the jury. All of my effort could go into the trial rather than working to appear to be someone I thought someone else wanted me to be.

There is greater freedom when you can focus on the task at hand without internal struggle. When you're trying to seem *as if* you are a certain way, it takes work. When you show up as you are, and in full acceptance of that, you can focus on the task at hand, and your ability to influence is magnified a thousand times.

Self-Acceptance and the Ability to Influence

"There is nothing noble in being superior to your fellow men. True nobility lies in being superior to your former self."
Ernest Hemingway

It is said that unless and until you love yourself, you cannot truly love anyone else. There is a similar truth in the art of persuasion. We cannot influence others without wholeheartedly embracing ourselves—knowing who we are and that we trust ourselves.

To try to create a comfortable life, we step into roles—father/mother, husband/wife, and employee/boss, and, in order to fit in, most of us subdue our true nature. We apply significant effort to play these roles according to society's view of what each one dictates. When we put so much energy into trying to become who we think we are supposed to be, it's easy to forget who we are. Or we can become so convinced that who we are will fail to meet expectations, we try to hide our true selves. We try to be the person others expect us to be.

Despite our best efforts to cover up, our true character will ooze out the sides of the masks and costumes that we wear. Whether we know it or not, people see us, especially the aspects we try to hide.

The roles we play in life may appear to have come upon us naturally. But when we look a little deeper, we may discover that the version of us that we present is not the same as who we were born to be.

Sometimes it's a traumatic event, like being ridiculed at school, or a problematic relationship that causes us to seek cover to protect ourselves from further injury. More often, the suppression of our true nature occurs subtly, over many years, starting from the first time we're corrected by our parents, and then continuing for decades. Tragically, many people live out entire lifetimes and never embrace their true nature. Meanwhile, the struggle to keep up the façade devours their life-force energy.

No matter how unpopular you fear your ideas and desires may turn out to be, in order to influence, you must go forward in complete confidence and have the internal consistency that says, "I am who I am, take it or leave it."

Few people have achieved that level of self-love and self-acceptance, because they are locked up in a prevailing sense of shame about who they are and what they want. Shame is the emotion that lies at the root of several limiting ideas:

self-doubt, embarrassment, feeling inadequate, or a fear of failure. At the core, these emotions and fears are all a product of concerns about how others see us.

The roles we play in life may appear to have come upon us naturally. But when we look a little deeper, we may discover that the version of us that we present is not the same as who we were born to be.

Our fear that others will reject us becomes a huge obstacle to influence. When you seek to influence, you need to be focused on your goal, not on yourself. When you apply energy toward avoiding shame or failure, your efforts are focused in the wrong direction.

No matter how hard you try to cover it up, your core personality comes through in every single thing that you do. You can try to change it. You can try to act as if you're someone else, or work like mad to try to make a certain impression, but as you do so, assume that others are going to perceive a mismatch as they hear and see through you.

Let's step back for a moment and think about influence. The goal is to alter someone else's course of action or behavior. You want them to do what you want them to do. If you look at it in the most simplistic way, you want them to allow you to direct them. Think about when you are driving on the road and the person ahead of you creeps into every intersection or slows to read every street sign. You can tell they are lost and need direction. You would not want to follow that person anywhere. The same is true of the people you wish to influence. If you lack confidence in who you are, their subconscious mind will send up a red flag warning them that you lack internal congruence. This hampers their ability to trust you to lead.

When you seek to influence, you need to be focused on your goal, not on yourself. When you apply energy toward avoiding shame or failure, your efforts are focused in the wrong direction.

If you are ashamed of yourself, people know. If you do not trust yourself, people know. Any time you speak, whether one-on-one or in front of a crowd, if you are not 100% accepting of yourself, people will assume that you are hiding something. Even if everything you say is 100% truthful, and you have zero awareness that you're withholding anything, if you are unconsciously trying to cover up some aspect of who you are, your audience will sense it, and they will react negatively to it. Sometimes it will come across as weakness or a lack of self-confidence. Other times it may be read as deceptiveness. However it manifests, they will have a nagging sensation that something about what you're saying is "off" or "not right." Unchecked, the impacts are devastating: you will lose the client or fail to make the sale. You will lose the team member or fail to realize your vision.

On the flip side, if you enter into a situation having mastered self-acceptance, people will sense consistency and reliability in you. They will feel they are able to trust you, and they will be far more likely to take the actions you want them to take. And they won't have to like you or approve of you to do it.

You may not believe that people will accept you with all of your flaws and issues. Maybe you're reading this and thinking, "Joe's feeding me a bunch of B.S.", but the more you accept yourself, the more universal acceptance you'll experience.

Whether you're aware of it or not, when it comes to accepting you, most people will follow your lead. You will never win over every single individual, but more people will embrace you when you embrace yourself. Everyone has personal aspects that they fear are "unacceptable." When you demonstrate your ability to embrace your own quirks and your own personality, others will derive both strength in their own self-acceptance and confidence in you.

Many of us believe we have a clear picture of who we are and what we want, but a true understanding of self requires you to understand not only your personal capabilities, dreams, and ambitions, but a clear view of your core character. Your character distinguishes you from every other person on this planet. It is a product of your natural tendencies and the sum total of everything in your life that you have experienced and learned.

You also need to be aware of the image you project. The way that you do what you do will always define who you are to those you encounter. If you lack this understanding, you will unintentionally create hesitancy due to your incongruencies. People will hesitate in their heart, and when confronted with a choice, they may find greater security in a path that is not the one you had in mind. By remaining consistent, solid in yourself, you minimize the forks in the road where people can choose to divert from your path.

You were born who you are, but you were not shaped overnight. In fact, if you are fifty, you were shaped in about 18,000 overnights. From the time of childhood, each of us has been taught "right from wrong." We have been told what we're good at and what we're not so good at, what we should do and what we shouldn't.

Unfortunately, many of the things you learned from others were just wrong, namely, anything that has caused you to suppress your true nature and your true self. Maybe you listened when you were told that you could not do something. Maybe you were convinced that you would be a failure at what you love because someone told you that you could never succeed.

Most of us learn not to take risks, *not* because we fear that we might fail, but because *we fear we might be criticized* for failing.

By remaining consistent, solid in yourself, you minimize the forks in the road where people can choose to divert from your path.

Think about all of the things people told you in the past that you still hear in your head. Admit where you've allowed those voices to suppress who you are. Acknowledge that to be the person you are meant to become, you can't continue to suppress your true self. The voices are wrong. Look past them and find your inner self. Your inherent superpowers are those elements of your character that allow others to find in you the traits that bring them the feeling of trust that makes them willing to follow.

Find Your Superpowers

"With great power comes great responsibility."
Uncle Ben to Spider-Man

Peter Parker was a tentative teenage boy. Compliant and eager to please, he suffered from the usual adolescent struggles. He lived with his beloved Aunt May and Uncle Ben and reluctantly did his chores and his homework every day. Then he was bitten by a radioactive spider, and his superpowers turned on: he gained Spidey sense and the agility to jump from building to building with ease. But Spider-Man had yet to be born.

At first, Peter chose to use his powers only for his own gain by engaging in a wrestling match for money. Later that night, when he saw a burglar being chased by a security guard, the guard called out to him and asked him to intercept. He refused. After all, he thought, it wasn't his concern, so he did what most people would do: nothing.

In a pivotal twist of fate, the same burglar later killed Peter's Uncle Ben. The personal loss hit him hard. It was only then that he heeded his late uncle's words and accepted the truth that, "With great power comes great responsibility." He appeased his own sense of guilt with a commitment to use his powers for good.

Spider-Man had arrived. A superhero was born.

Admirable, yes, yet it's worth noting that he chose to engage his superpowers fully only after he suffered the consequences of acting "normal." Ignoring our superpowers never ends well. Each of us has suffered the consequences of acting like everyone else: "normal" results. For most people, normal results are fine, but if your goal is excellence, normal results suck.

To be an effective influencer, you need to be willing to step out of "normal" and engage your superpowers. You have to be willing to allow "being nice" to yield to directness. Apathy must yield to initiative. And fear must yield to courage. No matter what opinions others may have of you, you must own the responsibility for the outcome of your actions and your decisions. Make them yours and be responsible for who you are and for your results.

Like Spider-Man, most of the superheroes in comic books and in movies started out as normal people with normal character traits and normal personal struggles. Then, after an alien plane crash or exposure to a laboratory chemical, each superhero developed a new set of powers. But when they were not acting in their roles as superheroes, they all struggled with everyday issues. It was how and when they used their powers that made them super.

You, too, are starting out as a "normal" person. Super-powers are nothing more than enhanced skills that all humans possess. Once you recognize and accept your inner strengths, you will be able to unlock all the superpowers you have. Not that you can jump from building to building, or run at the speed of light, but you can make the most of what you have and achieve great things, and you won't need a radioactive spider bite to do it. All you need to do is turn on the three superpowers that you already possess:

- Courage
- Perseverance
- Optimism

If you believe you lack any or all of these traits, you're mistaken. They are yours. They may be dormant or covered up by inhibitions and fears rooted in shame, but as soon as shame is no longer running the show, you will enhance your ability to persist; you will see challenges with optimism; and you will have the courage to do what you need to do to succeed.

Regardless of which traits you feel you possess right now, these are the three character traits required to be an effective influencer. If any of these traits are weak or are not apparent in you right now, you must cultivate them or give up hope of becoming an influential person. People are willing to follow someone who can take on a challenge and commit to victory, especially when they can see benefits in the outcome.

Influencers who possess the courage to act, remain steadfast in moving ahead despite difficulty, and tend to look on the more favorable side of setbacks, will shine as beacons of leadership. Your courage, perseverance, and optimism will translate into a safe bet for success that people will embrace with ease. Your commitment to the end goal will draw the people who share your vision nearer to you. They will feel your confidence as your resolve radiates from within. Combined, these three traits send a message that inspires people to believe that goals can be accomplished, challenges will be defeated, and eventual success is assured. Influence will easily follow.

Every superhero finds they have undiscovered powers waiting to emerge. These new powers become a source of additional energy. You have a unique combination of several other character traits that can provide you with abilities that will be yours alone, and you can use them to create your own personalized version of success. Let's have a look.

Below is a list of twenty character traits. As you read the list, consider which of these you express every day, which you express sometimes, and which you do not express but could be cultivated.

- Authentic
- Compassionate
- Conscientious
- Courageous
- Fair
- Forgiving
- Generous
- Honest
- Humble
- Integrous
- Kind
- Loving
- Loyal
- Optimistic
- Persevering
- Polite
- Reliable
- Respectful
- Responsible
- Self-disciplined
- Trustworthy

---

*Your courage, perseverance, and optimism
will translate into a safe bet for success that
people will embrace with ease.*

As you read through the above list, you will likely see that there are several traits that you can comfortably say fit your personality on most days.

Now let's look at a different list of traits. Again, consider which of these you express every day, which you express sometimes, and which you do not express but could be cultivated.

- Annoying
- Bullying
- Cynical
- Dishonest
- Distracted
- Egotistic
- Entitled

- Unsympathetic
- Ignorant
- Immoral
- Lazy
- Greedy
- Messy
- Neurotic

- Pessimistic
- Rude
- Selfish
- Shy
- Stubborn
- Thin-skinned
- Unreliable

Did you have trouble with either of these lists? Did you happily check off most of the traits in the first list and feel proud of how well you turned out? Were there any traits on the first list that you saw as beyond your capacity for "goodness"?

What about the second list? Did you skim it and reject all the traits as you muttered, "Not me, I was raised better than that"? Were there any traits you saw as beyond your capacity for being "bad"?

If you're like most people, you scanned the second list and either felt confident in concluding that you do not possess most of those traits, or you felt shame at the realization that, at least some of the time, you've exhibited every one of them. Quite possibly, you moved rapidly through the list because you feared you'd be embarrassed by what you see as your dark side, those parts of yourself that you prefer to keep hidden. If you continue to carry shame, those characteristics will hold you back. Choosing to be blind to your negative traits will cause you to remain trapped by your own effort to ignore your reality.

Or maybe you zipped through them thinking that you are better than that. Stop kidding yourself. I thought that at first, too. I was lying to myself and, if you believe that you're "too good" for any item on that list, you're lying, too. If you are feeling ashamed, you need to give that up too. Truth is, we all have all of these traits! We are human, and these are all human characteristics; thus, we all have the capacity to express them, and under the right circumstances, each one of us could.

Even though every one of these characteristics is routinely labeled as positive or negative, this is not the case. Not one of the traits on this list is inherently positive or negative. No trait should bear a label of good or bad. The value of all human character traits can be defined only by the context in which they are employed and the mindset of the one who expresses them. If a world leader blurts out state secrets at a social event, perhaps they're being honest, but if revealing the information threatens national security or the lives of its citizens, that honesty could be viewed as a negative trait.

The traits we've labeled as "positive" are not necessarily so in the wrong hands. Consider that while you may be hard pressed to associate any of the so-called positive traits with either Attila the Hun or Adolf Hitler, their followers would not agree with you. If you were a member of the Hunnic Empire, you would have described Attila as loyal and courageous. If you were a member of the Third Reich, you would attribute to Adolf Hitler the trait of perseverance. And, while his vision was cruel and inhumane, he was optimistic in his plans to succeed. Attila also was an optimist. He never entered a battle that he thought he would lose.

On the flip side, as we look at the traits that are generally viewed as "negative" we can see the same truth, that in in the right hands and in the right context, "negative" attributes can be extraordinarily powerful assets.

I think it is a safe assumption that neither Hitler nor Attila were globally well liked. I cannot fathom Attila the Hun caring whether or not anyone liked him, and by all accounts, Hitler had fewer than ten friends in his lifetime. Yet, despite both being unpopular loners, they were influencers. They offered to their followers a unifying vision. People loyally followed these men, did their bloody bidding, and died for them.

While my daughters may not have agreed when they were teenagers, I'm no tyrant like those guys. But I am in touch with my dark side: One of my superpowers is pessimism.

Like all superheroes, you can use your
hidden powers to give you energy and
a positive charge as you move forward.

As a trial lawyer, I spent my entire career expecting people to do something unpredictable that could derail me. Every day, I'd strategize to prepare for the worst. By always seeing the negative, or downside, ahead of time, I was ready for anything. Still am. Pessimism has been the source of all of my success, drive, and ambition. It has given me the ability to master my fears.

Do I allow pessimism to overshadow my optimistic side? No way! I expect to win. I use my pessimism to help me do it. Each trait can be used to benefit you and the people you lead. Every one of them can be used to influence. It is how you decide to view and express a trait that defines whether it is positive or negative. Put simply: in the right hands, all traits are positive.

As long as you hold optimism, perseverance, and courage as your three unshakable traits, you can lead anyone to accomplish anything.

If you perceive that you have a "negative" trait, look at the circumstances where expressing that trait could be helpful in terms of influence. If you look at all of your "negative" traits and find how they can be employed to help you, you can employ them as a positive force in your ability to influence. So-called "negative traits" are only disruptive to your vision if you allow them to overshadow the three essential traits. Cynicism is only a block to influence if it overshadows optimism. Entitlement isn't a problem unless it trumps perseverance. Shyness will never stop you unless you let it dampen your courage.

Even more exciting, you can express so-called "negative" traits to help you toward your goals in a very "positive" way.

"Negative" Trait		Or is it…?
Cynical	→	Evaluative
Distracted	→	Visionary
Conceited	→	Confident
Lazy	→	Efficient
Messy	→	Spontaneous
Neurotic	→	Conscientious
Pessimistic	→	Cautious
Stubborn	→	Determined
Shy	→	Observant
Thin-skinned	→	Perceptive

If you are really brave, go back to the main list of "negative traits" and circle the ones you still won't own, or you feel shame about. Write them on a piece of paper. Those are your dormant superpowers.

Like all superheroes, you can use your hidden powers to give you energy and a positive charge as you move forward. Know that your dreams are bigger and more powerful than any imagined limitation.

> *As long as you hold optimism, perseverance, and courage as your three unshakable traits, you can lead anyone to accomplish anything.*

Think about a challenge you're facing now. Take out the list of traits you're struggling to call your own. Determine which ones of those so-called negative traits you could activate in a "positive" way to help you influence the situation in your favor.

If you're still not sure, or even if you think you know, this next section is going to show you how to get some help to see yourself so you can turn up your influence superpowers to the max.

The "W.O.W.!" Factor and You

"Be yourself; everyone else is already taken."
Oscar Wilde

In 1992, I was working part-time as a magician at banquets and social events. At that point in my career, my act consisted of a series of routines that had been written and scripted by various other people. In performance, I had to deliver other people's words and phrases as if they were my own, and I worked hard to transition between tricks in such a way that the audience would experience a sense of consistency between them.

On one December evening, I finished a show at a large hotel and received a standing ovation. I smiled, thanked the audience, and exited the stage. As I packed my belongings and made my way to the car, I realized that I felt empty.

A major snowstorm had just begun, so I knew the ride home was going to be long. As I started the car, I reflected on the evening's show and the audience's reaction. I felt an intense sadness. I wondered what the heck was wrong with me. I had just gotten a standing ovation, and I hated myself for it.

As I drove through the blizzard, I continued to dissect my concerns. I wondered if my disappointment was because I knew the audience was showing appreciation for a blend of other's writings and performance styles. I was hiding behind the work of other people. I never showed them the real me.

I knew if I were going to continue performing, I needed to find my own voice. I needed to find out who I was and allow my true character to lead my performances; not a manufactured amalgamation. But how? I'd never scripted a magic show in my life, and I had no desire to do so.

I called a friend, Beth, to talk me through my cluttered thoughts. I knew that her knowledge and matter-of-fact personality would deliver the honesty that I needed.

I told her what had happened and how awful I felt.

Beth replied, "You have never really been happy performing magic, it is not what you are meant to do."

Our discussion continued with her critique of how I allowed the magic tricks to interfere with my personality and presentation skills. She insisted, "You are more entertaining when you interact with people. You don't need to hide behind tricks."

"So, are you telling me that I should stop amazing my audiences with my incredible, excitingly impressive feats of magic?"

"No, you should be a *mentalist*. Doing that, you will connect with people. That is where you would be the best."

"Mentalism is mind reading. I don't like it. It's not fun."

She retorted, "You will make it fun. Good night."

As I drove home, I considered what Beth had said. In my heart, I knew that she was right.

In the months that followed, I reached out to five other friends to ask them their impressions of me both on and off stage. I demanded brutal honesty and offered reassurance that I had a burning desire to improve and that hearing the bad was essential. The general consensus was that pulling rabbits out of a hat didn't fit my personality. They said that my strengths were in my understanding of human nature. They told me that they clearly saw that I derived the most enjoyment from playing *with* my audiences, not just *to* them.

Based on their feedback, I redirected my efforts and found that Beth's suggestion had been dead-on accurate. My natural gifts were more suited to mentalism and mind reading on stage. (After all, it was what I was doing when I picked juries and cross-examined witnesses in court.) I realized that by getting rid of the props and toys, I could be 100% me, and 100% present with my audience. This is the internal state that enables one to influence. Without a 100% level of self-knowledge and self-acceptance, I was merely mouthing words and in no position to move minds and hearts.

The hard part was the discovery. Once I began to journey down that road, it was easy to be consistent on stage because I wasn't pretending to be someone else. There was nothing to change. I no longer needed to avoid taking on the personality of the person who scripted each piece. Every segment of my show highlighted *my* character and was infused with *my* personality.

I was fortunate that my friends loved me enough to take the time to give me solid, hard criticism and honest feedback. I learned that everyone was unified in the thought that my old show's tone had been erratic, and my effort had come across as strained. I was doing cool tricks, but my personality was buried. Neither the magic nor the entertaining had enabled me to shine. I took a two-year sabbatical from performing. During that time, I studied mentalism, evaluated whether mind reading could be fun, and how I could make it so. I read and I wrote about psychic entertaining. I repeatedly read and reread my notes on the criticisms from Beth and the others. I searched to find a way to be myself on stage, using the good and the bad to be as real as I could be.

While I was embroiled in this inquiry, Marc Salem invited me to come see his Off-Broadway show at the West Side Theater in New York. A mutual friend had contacted us insisting that we should meet, so I went to the Big Apple. His show was captivating, and I saw why he was considered one of the best. Not only was he entertaining and good at what he did, but his persona was consistent and enjoyable to watch. It appeared that he was the real deal; he was not playing any roles on stage. He was just being himself.

I introduced myself. He shook my hand and said, "I have to talk to the people who bought tickets, but we are going to be friends for a very long time, so call me later."

Marc is now one of my closest friends. I have confirmed my beliefs that he is the same man on stage as he is in his living room. His stage persona is just a well-honed version of his everyday being. After meeting Marc, I surrendered to allowing myself to be myself, everywhere I show up. I realized the importance of not hiding who I am. I knew I could no longer waste energy mimicking someone else. I became determined that I was going to embrace all of me no matter what.

After implementing my new plan, I soon realized that my audiences were not just enjoying my show, they were enjoying *me*. The comments that I received after each performance became focused upon my presence and not upon tricks that I performed. Rather than getting lost in the bits, my personality flowed through the performances evenly and consistently. The audience got to know me. Nowadays, when I get a standing ovation, it is humbling and rewarding at the same time. I know that the audience has enjoyed my performance, but more importantly, I know that they have seen all of me and accepted me for who I am because I accepted me first.

As I advise business owners and entrepreneurs, I encourage them to drop all of their walls so that they can see themselves as the world sees them. They need to know how they are perceived by their employees, clients, and prospects. I encourage people to make a list of people that they trust; people who are good friends, or family members. Then approach these people and ask, "What do you see when you look at me? What image do I project?"

I encourage you to do the same. Once you know how others perceive you, and you can embrace the feedback, you will be in a better position to locate your superpowers and use your natural character to your advantage.

Sound good? Okay. Here's the rub. You must actively pursue getting the "bad news." You must reach out to those who know you best and ask and listen to what they have to say with all your senses.

Yes, I am now recommending that you complete this task. The results will change your world. If you are dealing with people who truly love you, their honesty will be enlightening and occasionally painful. But, as you've heard, no pain no gain. Let them know that you are there to learn and that you are willing to accept any feedback they may offer, but let them know you need honesty. Tell them how important their accurate perception is to your commitment to grow and be open to hear whatever they tell you.

As you prepare to see your true self, be ready to turn your sights inward and apply the W.O.W. Factor to yourself. Allow yourself to embrace the new things you will learn as you become the keystone on which people can rely as they move forward toward your goal.

Willingness

You must be willing to grow and improve. To embark on a journey of self-discovery, you have to be ready to learn about yourself. Many of us tend to take care of everyone around us and provide for the needs of others, but we rarely stop and take time for ourselves. Tell yourself that you are ready, willing, and able to proceed on this journey and see it through. What you will find on the other side is well worth any effort you expend. You are instrumental in everything that you do. Until you learn about all of yourself, you cannot expect to be the person that others will follow.

If you want to succeed at influence, you must know how other people perceive you. You cannot simply guess or make assumptions. You need to attain an accurate picture of how you come across. You have to want to know what other people think about you, and you have to be willing to listen and consider their opinions.

We all seem to think we know who are. We think we know what it is that makes us tick. But as an influencer, you need to know what about you makes others tick. What makes other people want to endear themselves to you, and what makes other people want to follow you?

Denying that a trait exists creates a weakness—a void in your perception—that prevents you from fully embracing yourself. You can't love everything about yourself unless you know everything about yourself.

I know that in my personal journey, I have found perceived positives. But, taking the "negatives" that people have pointed out and discovering how I can tap them to develop new strengths, has been exciting and rewarding. Whether I am on stage in front of hundreds, standing in front a jury of twelve, or working one-on-one with a business owner, I am always comfortable allowing my evaluative and driven personality to infuse everything that I do. (Yes, I noticed that I did not use the words cynical and egotistical.) In fact, when I am on stage performing, I fully embrace those parts of me and allow them to be a source of humor.

Other people are more inclined to see things in us and in our lives that we cannot see or that we simply deny. The people closest to you will be in the best position to point out the aspects of yourself that you have been conditioned to reject. Your "hidden" traits are blatantly obvious to those who know you. You will be finding the positive in it all anyway, so just listen! Hear and consider their opinions to liberate yourself.

Other people are more inclined to see things in us and in our lives that we cannot see or that we simply deny.

Openness

Be open to listening to the feedback. Listen intently and focus on their answers. Do not try to explain yourself or rationalize. The minute you act on the feeling that you need to defend yourself, you are doing yourself a great disservice. Recognize that the need for defensiveness and the desire for praise is your ego acting up. Do not let the opportunity get away by explaining yourself at all. Your words could cause them to temper their feedback or to alter their raw thoughts.

As you listen, be in the moment. Avoid distractions. Do not think about what you are going to do with the information. Consciously give yourself permission to be present and listen. Remember that their openness is as important as yours. To ensure that the discussion does not implode, make sure that you both understand the purpose of the dialogue. Occasionally, you may want to ask follow-up questions to get a deeper cut of their insight. But don't interrupt or try to defend yourself or correct their perception. It's theirs. Let it be.

At the outset, remind them that you have selected them because you respect them and appreciate their advice. Then be sure that they understand the purpose of the conversation. Respect will be the foundation of the trust that allows them to be honest. If you have chosen the right people, your betterment is the shared goal that will bind the two of you in the conversation. Consider this an exercise in your ability to influence, because it is in this conversation that you must inspire the other person to be forthright and give you the information you desire.

Wonder

Always be learning. Have the curiosity of a child. Use everything to grow. Recognize that everything that you hear, see, and experience is necessary for the achievement of your goals. Consider the process of evaluation as a master class in you. As people are speaking, you are learning things you would not otherwise know. You will often hear things that you knew but did not want to admit. Take it all in. While later, you may want to filter certain information, that is not a decision that you should make right away. Allow everything to enter your mind without judgment. Imagine your mind is like the pan used by a gold prospector. When he scoops a pan of dirt from the basin of the river, the miner does not pick and choose the dirt. He fills the pan and filters away the debris to find one single grain of gold. Allow your mind to take in all available information realizing that that small nugget of gold exists in the midst of all the dirt.

In all ways, be a student. When I began as a trial lawyer, I believed that the training I had received qualified me to be in a courtroom. After the first trial or two, I realized the vast difference between academia and reality. My ego was crushed, and I felt incompetent. I didn't intentionally put my ego aside; it collapsed under its own weight.

I walked into senior Judge Cherry's office to seek help. He was a retired judge who had earned a position of great respect. With a broken ego, I asked him to tell me what I was doing right and wrong. He welcomed me into his office, and his face lit up with excitement over the prospect of assisting me. At that moment, I was overwhelmed that this man would actually be interested. I dropped all of my defenses and sat on the edge of my chair listening and soaking in every word. He instructed me from his forty years of experience on everything that I was doing and educated me on how to become a better trial lawyer.

I felt like an artist learning at the feet of the master. I recognized that you can be as good as you want to be, but if you are open to take a lesson from a master who is better and more experienced than you, eventually the student will become the master. As I listened to Judge Cherry, I absorbed every word he spoke. Every time I tried a case in front of him, I set aside two to three hours to sit with him after the trial ended to take in everything he would give me. It allowed me to become a better lawyer, and concurrently, a better influencer.

Learning the truth about yourself can be the most threatening thing your ego will ever experience, but it is the most powerful thing for your self-confidence and ambitions. Once you understand and fully embrace who you are, you can unleash a flood of energy and a host of superpowers. All of your attention can focus on your message and enable you to influence others to help you toward achieving your goals. You no longer have to waste time or energy trying to be someone you are not. Since you already embrace what others see, you no longer have to worry about how other people perceive you. You already know, and you're fine with it.

From this space you're empowered to take on the next element, and guide others to embrace your vision.

CHAPTER 6

Define the Roles

"I think it would be terrific if everybody was alike."
Andy Warhol

From the first time Bob, a Yellow Pages rep, walked into my office in 2000, I told him in no uncertain terms my goals and my budget, and I added one stringent condition: "If you make me an offer that's even one dollar over budget and doesn't match my goals, I'll happily escort you out of my office and you'll never get an appointment with me again."

We then discussed my business and my budgetary constraints. Once he had heard enough, he left and put together a proposal within the parameters I'd set. I signed up at $1,500 a month.

Over the years that followed, as Google's influence grew and the Yellow Pages waned, every six months Bob showed up at my office and each time I cut the budget, until 2014 when Yellow Pages advertising became pointless.

That time, when he came to see me, I told him, "Bob, I love ya', but I can't advertise in your book anymore." Bob told me that his goal was to be my advertising guy, not my advertising salesman. And then he proceeded to ask questions and to listen. He listened long enough to understand what I wanted and why.

Bob was gracious. "I understand your position. Do you want to have any presence at all?"

I said, "No, but I'll sign a $100 a month contract because it's you."

Bob looked at his computer, played with the listing options for a moment and said, "Are you okay at $103?"

I laughed and signed the contract for a one-line ad in an obsolete book for $103 per month.

Even though I was probably his smallest account, Bob continued to show up for our bi-annual meetings, and he kept me abreast of the company's progress toward internet capability. He made sure I was educated as to the services available and, more importantly, he made sure he knew what was happening in my life and business. Bob became an integral part of my marketing team.

Early in 2017, just after the sixteenth anniversary of our relationship, Bob came to me with an internet-based advertising solution that was a perfect fit for my needs and I signed a new contract for $2,000 a month.

Bob kept me interested and engaged. He had always paid attention to my needs and suggested a role change into which we could both easily transition.

I can assure you that if Bob had not listened to me in the first place, been my advisor, and stayed committed to the welfare of my business all those years, it never would have even occurred to me to use the company that handled my phone-book ads for help with my internet marketing. His consistency in demonstrating genuine interest in my needs and persistent listening influenced me to happily sign a rather substantial deal that I anticipate continuing into the foreseeable future.

To influence someone, you have to get them to trust you. Warranted or not, people will trust you more if they believe that you understand their point of view. People who believe you understand them are more inclined to make the leap from resistant to willing.

Getting people to be willing to do what you want them to do is about a meeting of the minds. Both their mind and yours need to be aligned. Ultimately, the connection between you and the other people is what is going to carry you across the finish line, but the connection must begin at the starting line. How you relate to someone from the very beginning is paramount. I do not believe that there is a checklist of right and wrong questions or statements that you need to make to begin. It is about how you approach the encounter, and how you approach it is rooted in how you think about it.

If you focus on asking the "right" questions, or if you try to recall a checklist of things you need to say, the magic of the moment will be lost. Allow the connection to be genuine. Allow yourself to engage in a sincere dialogue. That is when the magic of a real connection happens. When people are able to connect with you whether one-on-one or in a group, they are poised to receive your message. If you appear insincere or false, your message, no matter how powerful, will fall on deaf ears.

Clarify Your Role in the Vision

"If somebody thinks they're a hedgehog, presumably you just give 'em a mirror and a few pictures of hedgehogs and tell them to sort it out for themselves."
Douglas Adams

At the beginning of any initial encounter, you are a mystery to other people. When you speak, the first thing people try to figure out is the context of the relationship. "Why is this person speaking to me? Why are they in my life at this moment?" They are searching to figure out what the roles are. The answer they find is based on the role each of you plays in the other's life. Maybe you are a boss and they are an employee, or you are a sales rep and they are a buyer. Maybe this person entered your life as a student and you are the teacher. As soon as you encounter a new person, they subconsciously seek a way to categorize the connection and try to figure out your role and theirs. It is at this moment that you have a powerful opportunity, because the one who defines the roles controls.

When you assume a role that supports your desired outcome and vision, those you lead will feel at ease. The moment they understand and embrace your role, they find theirs, and they are already following your lead. You have dictated the course of the relationship from the start. By defining the roles, you are positioned to dictate the course of the mission.

Even if you've never led in this way, you have already experienced this as a follower. For example, you never needed to be told that the teacher was in charge of the classroom. You just knew. You knew by their position at the head of the class. You knew by the way they spoke. You knew by the way they acted. The teacher asserted their role, and you followed. Sometimes you focused. Sometimes you were unruly. But you were always the student.

While you may take for granted that the teacher would be in an authority role, the teacher set the tone for the relationship. We can all remember that one teacher who tried to be at our level. The one who showed movies, ignored homework, and gave out easy As, so his students would like him. For me, it was a high school chemistry teacher. With long, greasy red hair and an unkempt beard, "Ott" talked to us as if he were trying to be one of the cool kids, and it set the tone and direction of the class. I remember the movies, the idle conversation, but I learned nothing about the periodic table or sodium chloride. In his class, we were all equals, and we got nothing accomplished.

---

*By defining the roles, you are positioned
to dictate the course of the mission.*

Mr. Carl, on the other hand, was the classic authoritarian teacher. Sure, we hated him, because he was stern and cold, but we learned. He made the roles clear every day with his take-no-prisoners approach. When we got a test back with good grades, this seriously angry man smiled. He didn't smile often. But when he did, we felt important. We felt proud. We were kings.

Whoever defines the roles guides the course of the conversation. Roles define the rules of the relationship; therefore, if you create the roles, you create the rules. The existence of roles helps to create stability by defining the associated responsibilities. By creating the appropriate role structure to the situation and helping the people on your team understand and adopt their roles, you are in a much better position to lead people toward your goal.

People have a subconscious need to define roles because they need to know where they belong in the big picture. They find security in understanding their role because there is security in knowing one's responsibilities. When you create a space, and show a person where they fit in, it is much easier for them to know what is expected, and most people will naturally attempt to meet those expectations.

Before you go into any meeting, ask yourself, "Who does this person need me to be to take my direction?" Figure out the answer to that question and you will be in the driver's seat.

Early in my career as a defense lawyer, I was the court-appointed attorney for Lenny, a man charged with armed robbery. The court administrator warned, "You are the fourth lawyer we are sending this case to. Lenny asked the court to fire the first two, and he punched the third when he heard the plea deal. We think you can handle him."

I replied with a subdued "No problem," while inside I relished the opportunity.

The next day, I picked up the file and reviewed everything before visiting Lenny at the prison. He had been charged with walking into three mini-markets, pulling out a shotgun, and demanding all the money in the register and "...a couple of Fireball jawbreaker candies." I saw that he had confessed. In addition, the checkout clerks at each robbery had provided a positive ID. Still, he said he was innocent, and yes—you read it right—*he had confessed!* In the file I saw that the prior attorney had negotiated a deal for five years in prison if Lenny pled guilty. It looked to me like a sweet offer. He should have been grateful, but instead he had punched the lawyer in the face? Why?

As Lenny came down the hallway to the visitor's area, he strutted with the bravado that you would expect from a hard-core con. Weighing a total of about 150 pounds, I guessed that his badass attitude made up 140 of them. I concluded he would only communicate with me if I defined roles he could relate to.

If I acted as the "lawyer" to his "client," he would punch me, too. So I defined new roles. He was a street thug, and I was a bigger street thug.

He entered the visitor's area, and with no introduction, I told him to sit down. "Your file says you were offered five years..."

He jumped from his seat and began an incoherent rant that lasted several minutes. I sat still and watched him as if he were a gnat bounding around the room until he wore himself out.

"Sit down," I ordered.

He froze. "You ain't like them other lawyers, is you?"

"No." Then I sat, my gaze fixed on his eyes.

He broke the silence. "What d'you think I should do?"

"I assume you don't want the deal. You punched Attorney Smith. You are pissed. You know you are going to be convicted, and you see no difference between serving five or fifteen years. I see that. Trial is a long shot, but it is your only hope. So there is no way are you going to plead guilty. I got you. You aren't going to give up. All you want is a fair trial." I paused, "Are we good?"

"Yeah," he sat back in his seat and relaxed. "I'm glad I punched Smith. You ain't gonna sell me out. Now I got a lawyer who gets me."

He was where I needed him; I was in his head, and he wanted me there. He understood a badass attitude. I was in a role he could relate to.

His acceptance of my role allowed me to open the door. He felt understood, and that left him feeling free to give me the ability to do my job (without getting punched). He found comfort in my resolve. Had I not been so certain, he would not have accepted my position so readily. By taking a role he was familiar with, he related to me and gave me what the streets taught him to do when dealing with a bigger thug: give respect.

He felt important because I was willing to step into his world. I did not try to drag him into the "lawyer" world. I allowed him to willingly follow me into my world as the attorney/client relationship developed and we readied for trial.

Had I gone along with the expected roles, I would've been the lawyer and he would have been the client, and, like my predecessor, I would have received a punch to the jaw. Had I allowed Lenny to dictate his role as the bigger street thug, he would have been dominant, and I would have had no authority to gain his cooperation. But, by defining the roles as I did, I represented him effectively and did not get punched in the jaw. The role I cast for myself created a feeling in him of trust and respect. It was a role he could relate to, and he made the choice to follow my lead. The role I assigned him allowed me to get through to him and influence him to accept my direction.

Although we both knew he was going to lose at trial, and he did, he followed my lead for the remainder of the case. After his conviction, another lawyer appeared with him at sentencing. He got ten years; it was less than expected. He told the new lawyer to "Thank Mr. Curcillo for giving me a fair trial."

Let's look for a moment at the deeper problem that existed in my meeting with Lenny. The last time Lenny had agreed with anyone was when he confessed to the police. That agreeable "yes" response is what landed him in jail. In his mind, his willingness to be agreeable and admit to the crime is what had stripped him of his liberty. Lenny did not have a problem with the fact that he had committed a robbery. He had a problem with getting caught. In his mind, he only got caught because he said "Yes, I did it." He was not inclined to agree with any authority figure ever again. He needed trust. He would never have trusted me had I not stepped into his shoes and saw the world through his eyes.

Personally, I would not want to do one day in jail. So, to me, the difference between five and ten years is a lifetime. But from Lenny's perspective, it made no difference. I had never spoken to Lenny before that first meeting in prison, but I have spoken to hundreds of guys like Lenny in my lifetime. I understood his mindset. The plea offer had insulted his pride. I saw that. Once he saw that I understood him, he granted me permission to lead.

Choose Your Role Based on the Needs of Others

In order to get someone to buy into your vision, you have to figure out beforehand who they need you to be in order to follow you. Giving your audience a few moments of consideration allows you to reflect upon which role best suits the situation so you can provide a space for them to voluntarily get with your program. You want other people to accept the role that you have in mind for them, and you want them to be happy in it. It is from this space that you have the most power to influence. Skip this step, and you won't get any buy-in, only backlash.

During college, I spent a summer working in construction. On one hot day, after a morning of running a jackhammer, I was called to the atrium because the building owner had come on site to personally thank the work crew. We were all covered in sweat and a fine coating of grey concrete dust.

The owner stood on the second-floor railing and spoke to us from above the construction area. From the moment he stepped upon his pristine pulpit, he sent the entire moment spiraling downward. There could be no recovery. It may have been his custom-tailored Italian silk suit, or it may have been the high ground from which he spoke, or it may have been the attractive woman next to him who handed him a towel to wipe the concrete dust from his hands but, whichever it was, we rejected him in the role he had created. The "precious prince" did not understand or respect us, and we returned the favor. His afternoon address was mimicked and mocked by the crew the entire summer.

Had the owner chosen his role based our needs, coming down to the construction area and standing among us instead of speaking from above and looking down on us, he would have been able to influence us to heightened levels of enthusiasm and productivity. Had he taken such an approach, we would have embraced his remarks more easily, because we would have felt like he respected us. And he probably would have gotten the outcome he wanted. But it was not to be. We returned to work with the same lack of enthusiasm that we'd had before he spoke, but with a new twinge of resentment added on. A huge opportunity blown due to not choosing the correct role for the circumstance.

Think about it: Nobody gets enthusiastic about a forty-hour week hugging a jackhammer. But had the owner chosen a role that demonstrated that he respected us, we could have received his "thank you" and become even more dedicated to his vision. Now, his vision would never be ours.

Communicating what your team is supposed to do provides a sense of direction, but showing them how their role is vital to the big picture is the only thing that will create buy-in. People need to know that, however small, their part is recognized and valued as a vital component of the whole. Whether it is a waitress walking onto the floor of a restaurant, a salesman walking into a sales call, a maintenance worker with a mop, or a soldier going into battle, if you want a person to do their best, they must believe that you respect them and their contribution and that their role is essential to the success of the entire venture.

To help you figure this out, pay attention to the situation and context of the relationship. Ask yourself, "What role does this person need to see in me so that they will trust me and allow me to influence them?"

When you are sizing people up, use all of your observation skills. Listen to them; watch them. If someone needs to feel like they are your equal, or they need to feel like they are your student, shedding the title of "boss" may just move you that much closer to your end goal. This assessment can be accomplished in a matter of seconds, or it may occur during a conversation. Many times, the situation will dictate the best role for you to take.

Try this: when you look at someone on your team, see them as today's most valuable player. Think of them as indispensable. Then, think about what you need to influence them to do. Out of all possible roles, which is most likely to get them to take the action you need them to take?

As you contemplate the role you must adopt in dealing with that person, realize that the amount of insight you have into their needs will determine how effective your chosen role will be. One thing I know for sure, the authoritarian telling them that they are nobody and can be easily replaced and they'd better do it or else, is the least effective. When you belittle people, they will have no purpose. They will become disengaged.

Cast Those You Want to Influence in Their Roles

"Good evening, ladies and gentleman. My name is Orson Welles. I am an actor. I am a writer. I am a producer. I am a director. I am a magician. I appear onstage and on the radio. Why are there so many of me and so few of you?"
Orson Welles

Whoever assigns the roles controls the conversation. One of the most impressive examples was when my client, John, asked that I accompany him, as his corporate counsel, to a meeting with a corporation seeking to acquire his company. John, the CEO, had wanted the sale and had built a relationship with the negotiator, but his wife, Diane, was an equal shareholder and held the title of CFO. Despite her role on paper, she was unhappy that John had never included her in any business decisions. He had no choice but to include her now. She didn't want to sell, and he didn't want to try to force her into it and then have to live with her resenting him for the rest of his life. We sat at the table across from the corporate officers. I sat to John's right and Diane sat to his left

The acquiring corporation began discussions by summarizing how they'd first met my client the year prior. They rehashed some of the situations where they had already worked together and created revenue streams for my client. Diane and I simply listened. John continued to agree and laugh as they shared war stories. In fact, it was very clear that the corporate negotiator had spent over a year listening to my client's needs and wants. I remember thinking, "They know more about John and Diane than these two know about themselves."

Whoever assigns the roles controls the conversation.

I realized then that this was not casual reminiscing. This was an intentional and well-thought-out presentation to remind my clients that a relationship began over a year prior to the negotiation meeting. Or, as I saw it, this was the point man from the acquiring corporation assigning roles. The negotiator joked and chided John about some of his antics over the course of their friendship. The joking flowed back and forth and, by focusing on John's affable nature, had put John in the role the point man needed him to be in for this meeting. John was the comic relief, and he was loving it.

Of course, John's role was the easiest. The negotiator knew that his vision reflected exactly what John wanted, and John was visibly pleased. To the contrary, Diane appeared stoic and unimpressed.

As I watched Diane, I realized that they were not only acknowledging John's relationship with the major corporation, but they were paving a road for Diane to see the positive direction that they had already traveled. Diane was being groomed to accept the role the negotiator had in mind for her.

The tone of the conversation then shifted as they began to go over some of the financial data. They mapped out the amount of money they intended to invest in the company, and they presented reports, graphs, and charts projecting the heights the company could reach if the acquisition occurred.

The negotiator explained to Diane the more active role they envisioned for her in the new company. It was clear that the negotiator knew Diane's needs. He had learned ahead of time, through John, that Diane wanted more control.

They suggested a sizable salary and benefits package, and told her that after the acquisition, she would have a vital role in running the company. She became increasingly excited. And then he dropped the cherry: she would have the power to make decisions and contribute her insights. She would be the Queen. By the time the presentation was over, he had given Diane the professional affirmation she craved.

In retrospect, I now realize that the negotiator had also pre-determined a role for me and had put me in my role first. I had been neutralized.

For the negotiator to accomplish his aims, I had to be non-essential. By asserting his rapport with Court Jester John and elevating Diane to the status she craved as Queen, I automatically was relegated to Eunuch. Once he had inspired Diane with her role in his vision, he turned to John and said, "I would like to review where I see you in the next ten years." The negotiator then rose from his seat and walked to our side of the table. He stood behind Diane and said to John, "It will be easier to walk you through this if the plan is in front of you."

He then reached between the couple placing the compensation proposal in front of John. Diane stood up and moved one seat away. She gave her seat at her husband's left side to the negotiator. John was predisposed to sell, and by moving to another chair, Diane had just signaled her approval.

I watched the corporate team lean back and relax as the negotiator sat in the newly vacated seat. It was clear that she had surrendered the seat of power at her husband's side, because she had accepted everything she heard. I knew then that my failure to define the roles first had made it impossible for me to execute what they had asked me to do before the meeting, which was to review the agreement and advise them before they signed. I tried to step in and asked my clients to take a break, but it was too late. They declined and said, "No, this is good."

They were both all in.

The deal went through, and it all worked out fine. It wasn't a bad deal, but the point is that because I had no part in defining the roles, I had no influence.

Changing Predefined Roles

"All the best performers bring to their role something more, something different than what the author put on paper. That's what makes theatre live. That's why it persists."
Stephen Sondheim

One of the most difficult things to do from a management standpoint is to walk into a situation with an existing team that's been precast, meaning that each person has been in their position for a while and everyone is certain that they know their role, and the only role in question is yours.

People get set in their ways and tend to resist change. Maybe they will tell you directly, but more likely you will know by their actions. Regardless of whether the team is motivated or not, when you come in, if you want to make them your team, you'll need to redefine some roles.

One of the most difficult situations I have encountered involved a government office. When I first attempted to resolve the problem I was informed that the office was funded through a grant, and there was concern that if the office did not come into conformity with the standards of the grant guidelines, funding would be in jeopardy. Simply put, the office staff was resistant to management and was failing to produce measurable results.

My initial investigation revealed that the staff was well-trained and professional, but simply did not want to answer to anyone that they believed was a threat to their independence. It became clear that the only viable option was to find a way to restructure and bring into line the disgruntled and rebellious personalities and attitudes.

The office had received the nickname "Siberia." Dedicated to long-term white-collar crime investigations, the work was tedious and boring. It was well known that this was the place where supervisors sent field agents when they wanted them fired but didn't want to deal with the paperwork. The staff had struggled with management in their previous positions, and they brought their angst and rebellion to Siberia. They all felt that they knew the best way to do their jobs, and any effort to manage them was rebuffed. The staff was biased against any outside demonstration of authority.

Individually, the investigators possessed a great deal of valuable institutional knowledge. To clean house and get rid of everyone would have slowed an already arduous investigative process. At times, the investigations required several years of analyzing boring financial data before arrests could be made. Due to the long-term nature of the investigations, the number of arrests and indictments was low, and, since it was slow, measuring results was difficult. However, the parent office needed to be able to report that progress was being made or lose funding.

The investigators were prone to filing reports containing their conclusions absent the facts that supported them. They were so defensive that a simple request for more explanation of their investigative conclusions was received as an insult to their competence. Management needed to get the worker's cooperation to be able to effectively track the assignment and completion of investigation reports to show that forward progress was being made. But how?

Initially, I tried to establish the traditional roles of boss/employee. When that failed, I moved from coach/team, to team member/team member, to friend/friend. Failed. Failed. Failed. They were not buying any of it. They knew they could not be easily fired. I knew that they should not have been fired because they had the institutional knowledge the office needed; their years of knowledge were necessary to the unit's success.

This was one of the most difficult and volatile managerial situations that I had ever encountered. Any time they had been accused of failure in the past, they blamed management. They had become accustomed to avoiding any relationship that would allow management to develop a relationship with them individually or as a group. They refused to drop their guard and focused on proving that they were right and I, as the outsider, was wrong.

I decided to try one more role. It had to be extreme. I allowed them to be the heroes they needed to be, and I became the villain.

Contrary to my norm, I maintained an unengaging presence. I holed up in an office and limited my interactions to only direct business matters. I avoided all social contact and trivial water-cooler interactions. I assigned work via memos so they knew everything was in writing. Every so often, I would emerge from my office to discipline someone. Other than that, I remained in my office—the villain's lair.

Once I began to issue directives and written disciplinary warnings, the employees realized that I was fighting back. Negotiation was no longer an option. The documentation sent a clear message that they either did their jobs, providing the detail as requested, or they would be terminated. They soon began performing in a manner that was consistent with the written goals of management. The staff wanted to beat the villain so badly that—as the heroes—they were doing exactly what I wanted them to do: fight back by proving their worth.

After several months, I watched patiently as members of the staff realized that getting rid of me was impossible. But, more importantly, they realized that my goals were not as bad as they had fantasized. One by one they came around. They began to request meetings and privately worked with me on their reports. Each met with me in their own time. I let them know that neither I nor management held the past against them, and that I was there to support them.

We discussed their acceptance of my role as team leader, and my willingness to accept each of them as an essential team member with a clean slate.

It was then that I finally had the buy-in I needed to switch roles again and join them as a member of an empowered team. The whole office got into the team member/team member state that I believe it was intended to be. The ship righted itself and it sailed smoothly. Becoming the common enemy was one of the toughest roles I ever took on, but it worked better than I had imagined.

Sometimes assuming a role is easy, sometimes it's hard. If you want to influence people to do what you want them to do, you have to do what you have to do. Allow the roles that you create to give you an opportunity to hold the primary position of influence in the relationship.

Allow the roles that you create to give you an opportunity to hold the primary position of influence In the relationship.

CHAPTER 7

Getting to Us

"Then from far away across the world he smelled good
things to eat, so he gave up being king of the wild things."
Maurice Sendak,
Where the Wild Things Are

Getting to us is about enrolling people into an idea so grand that it transcends self-interest, and so appealing that they fall in love with it. Once this is accomplished, the need to motivate or influence evaporates, and as long as you keep everyone devoted to the vision, you will have a team that propels itself toward your goals.

My father was a master carpenter. When asked what he did for a living, he was quick to say he built the Northeast Philadelphia neighborhoods. And it was true. Over the extent of his fifty-year-long career, he'd had a hand in building over forty thousand homes. If pressed for more details, he would not tell you he was a woodworker. He did not say he hit nails with a hammer. He drove a lot of nails; but that was only the daily grind. He would tell you he built homes for families to grow in. He gave people a place to call their own.

When a person, any person, has the awareness that their work is making a contribution toward a great achievement that surpasses anything that they could accomplish as an individual, and it's one that they believe in, they will grab hold of that opportunity and bring their grandeur to its fruition.

---

*People crave a sense that they are
an integral part of a noble cause.*

One of the most overlooked traits of people in the workforce is the basic need to feel a sense of worth. Pride in who they are. Pride in what they do. Everyone wants to hold the belief that they are making a difference. That even when they are gone and forgotten, some element of their work will have left a permanent mark upon the world. Simply put: people crave a sense that they are an integral part of a noble cause.

The way to do this is to create a noble vision for your company that allows your workers to see how every job, no matter how mundane or low-skill, is making a vital contribution to it. It is at this moment that you move from "you and me" to "us."

This chapter will introduce the key concepts that make this possible.

1. Make the Vision Clear
2. Draw Them in, Don't Drag Them
3. Be Present

Make the Vision Clear

*"A rock pile ceases to be a rock pile the moment
a single man contemplates it, bearing within
him the image of a cathedral."*
Antoine de Saint-Exupéry

The opening move to "getting to us" is to create the unifying vision and then communicate it. If it's designed correctly, everyone on your team will be able to see their role in it. If you hire the right people, everyone on your team will be excited to be a part of it. In order for that to happen, you have to know what the big picture looks like. If you want someone to embrace your vision, you've got to show them what they're hugging. Imagine what it will look like being carried out, and what it will look like when it's done.

The main criteria are: it must be bigger than your company, bigger than your self-interest, bigger than anyone on your teams. One key question you can ask yourself: "what is this company capable of doing to make the world a better place?"

Be crystal clear about how your vision will change the world. This can be on any scale, from bringing joy to someone's day, to giving the world tools to change humankind, to saving lives.

Go Big or Go Home

"You're gonna need a bigger boat."
Martin Brody (Roy Scheider), *Jaws*

When your vision is bigger than you, bigger than your team, bigger than your entire company, it lets people know that what you are creating together is important and you cannot do it alone. In many businesses, the vision is too small. When your vision is too small, it is also usually too narrow for workers to see how they are essential to it.

Many companies fear letting on to workers that their role holds any importance beyond "getting it done." What they fail to recognize is that a person who sees themselves in a key role in furtherance of a noble cause will be more engaged, put in more effort, and expect less in return than one who is reminded every day that they are unimportant and easily replaced.

When people see themselves as drones bringing in profits and glory for another, they are very unlikely to invest their heart and soul into the mission. The bigger the vision, the more noble the cause, the more they feel excited to do whatever is needed to propel it, and the more they will see their vital contribution to it. People want to know that they can change the world for the betterment of everyone, not that they can change the world for *you*.

The unifying vision inherently conveys to others that they are necessary; how you realize the vision is by everyone doing their job to keep the company going so it can deliver on its promise. In this way, tasks are no longer merely tasks, but steps toward a better world.

When people are fully enrolled in your vision, they will have the ability to flourish and find purpose in all they do. When you create a vision that people can believe in, their belief that they are contributing to a greater plan will fall in line as well. Being elevated to a higher calling and holding the belief that one is serving the greater good is the foundation of self-satisfaction. The feeling of power that comes with nobility and purpose leads to the drive to do more. People are motivated when they feel like they can improve their lives or serve a higher calling. Motivation is a natural outgrowth of being inspired. When you inspire others with opportunity, that is the easiest way to motivate. Whether people are inspired by self-interest or a noble cause, inspiration is the best motivator. If you help someone find a reason to act, you have motivated them. In persuasion, if you give them a reason to do what you want, they will do what you want. But it must be the right reason. It has to have meaning to the person. The more you can help an individual connect your vision to their needs, the more likely they are to join in and work to solve your problem with you.

Certainly, financial gain can be a great motivator, but in the long run, people need to feel as if they are receiving something of value that benefits their goals. We have all been told that money cannot buy happiness. Money is temporary.

In order to influence someone, they need to be offered something that they need or want. If you recognize what they value, and work into the plan a way for them to have it, you can ignite their desire to participate and open the door for them to gain a feeling of satisfaction in doing so. In turn, they will be far more motivated to give you what you want in exchange for what you have given to them.

When people perceive your vision as their potential path to be a part of something that will give them meaning, they will be more ready to find meaning in the work they are doing.

Create a vision that is so big that the vision stands as an invitation to the world to come, join us, and let's be great together. The bigger the vision, the bigger the table, and the bigger the growth your company will see.

Draw Them In, Don't Drag Them

"The clever cat eats cheese and breathes down
rat holes with baited breath."
W. C. Fields

When you suddenly pull a dog's leash, the dog digs in and pulls back. If you show a dog a bone, he'll go toward it. If a dog hears the call of its beloved owner, i.e., its highest calling in life, the dog will run toward him or her with zeal. The same is true for people. If someone feels that they are being forced to do something, they will resist and become defensive. Nobody wants to be compelled to go in one direction or the other. The exercise of free will is the greatest liberty that anyone possesses. It's the one power even God doesn't interfere with, so why would you think taking it away is going to make them want to work harder for you? You can offer them a "bone" in the form of a paycheck, and they will perhaps be excited for a while, but they will grow tired of chasing the same bone. They will want a new bone with more meat on it.

Yet, give a person a cause, an idea they fall in love with, and they will be loyal and eager to please beyond any level you can accomplish with coercion or bribes.

The best outcome for a leader is when you lead your team to inspired action. When you can move someone to the point that they leap into action carried by a feeling of, "I'm excited to be part of this, this is our work, this is for the betterment of everyone!" you have found your unifying vision.

As of January 2018, the employment page on the Apple website promises jobseekers, "The people here at Apple don't just create products—they create the kind of wonder that's revolutionized entire industries." The vision assures the would-be applicants a role in a large, innovative big picture. It draws to Apple people who want to find their place in the stars.

Amazon offers jobs saying, "We're a company of pioneers. It's our job to make bold bets, and we get our energy from inventing on behalf of customers. Success is measured against the possible, not the probable." And Microsoft offers the lure of empowerment with, "Each of our jobs has clear requirements for success but lots of room to push boundaries and grow."

The vision you create has to be enticing and inviting, but simplicity is the key. A big promise to allow people to make a difference does not need to be complicated. A few words can speak volumes and lead to major influence.

The many hotels in which I have stayed all have one thing in common: little cards in the bathroom encouraging me to save water, save the planet, and reuse my towels. In my room at the Nittany Lion Inn at Penn State, there was a door hanger with a picture of a little bear cub and a waterfall. The picture was cute and appealing. The message told me I can help the hotel save water and save Earth's freshwater supply. Also, I can save the water supply from contamination by helping the hotel to use less detergent.

Clearly, the suggestion to reuse towels to save the planet is an inviting message. It encouraged me to be part of a very big picture. If the hotel put on the card: "help us save on overhead and cleaning costs…", I don't think the message would have been so enticing.

Since these cards appear in nearly every hotel, I feel safe to conclude that they are effective. While I am not disputing the fact that some hotels truly do care about our environment, the message is clearly designed to benefit the hotel by lowering laundry costs with an environmental kicker.

The message offers a way to have a global impact, but the action required on the part of the guest is minimal. The reuse of towels is easy enough to sway, if only for that one stay, the hardest of non-environmentally conscious hearts.

It is astonishing that this effective message appears on a tiny card. The effectiveness clearly supports the notion that the process of influence can occur in less than 150 words and a few seconds to read. Persuasion is not a matter of time; it is a matter of impact.

A Vision People Can Love is the Greatest Influencer

"Love is life. All, everything, that I understand, I understand only because of love. All is bound up in love alone."
Leo Tolstoy

Help your teams fall in love with the vision. Make it so inspiring that each person would feel disappointed if they didn't get to participate in its fulfillment. People want to know that what they bring to the table is valued, and that they are in the right place. People will work for leaders who give their lives meaning.

This feeling can be achieved when people love doing their jobs, being philanthropic, or joining a cause of some kind. People do not join causes, such as fighting to protect the environment, for financial gain. People are motivated when they feel as if they are attaining a higher calling or rising to a level of nobility that allows them to feel fulfilled. Fulfillment comes from the sense of contribution to a vision that they deem as important. When the vision that you offer is embraced as important, people will be more inclined to be motivated toward that goal by their instinct to contribute to the greater good.

They Don't Have to Love You to Love Your Vision

"You can dream, create, design and build the most wonderful place in the world, but it takes people to make the dream a reality."
Walt Disney

One of the great benefits of a unifying vision is that it transcends personality conflicts. Some of the most successful companies had CEOs with difficult personalities, but their unifying vision was so inspiring they were able to hold on to top performers and dominate their respective markets. Jeff Bezos, founder of Amazon, is one case in point. As a boss, Bezos has been known to verbally assault his team with phases such as, "Why are you wasting my life?" and, "I'm sorry, did I take my stupid pills today?"

Yet, his unifying vision for Amazon—"to raise the bar across industries, and around the world, for what it means to be customer focused"—has rallied his ever-growing team (341,000 employees as of this writing) into fulfilling that commitment. Bezos is who he is. He has high demands because they are in line with his lofty goal. He has set his standards and is unapologetic about what he wants. He does not have to cozy up to people to get them to perform. He is so committed to his vision that those around him are assured success because he yields to nothing, and they know he will certainly not yield to failure.

He is also unapologetic for his behavior and attitude. As I have said elsewhere, you don't have to be Mr. Nice Guy. In fact, when you start to be too nice and you start sucking up to your employees, they will become very comfortable. When people become comfortable and content in their place, they have no incentive to leave that place; they will stagnate and do nothing that requires effort. Complacency is never the mother of motivation. If the horse knows that the water is always going to be there, it will only drink when it suits it to drink. You can inspire people to achieve by letting them know that their role is important to the outcome of the endeavor. When they can play that role with freedom and comfort within the confines defined by the role you have scripted for them, they know what they have to do to contribute to the overall success. If they love your goal, they will love their role in it.

I know of one Amazon employee who has moved up through the ranks of management. He began his career on the floor of a distribution center and has moved upward from there. He describes the work as grueling and fast-paced, yet cannot imagine working for a better company. He feels personally responsible for his role in the fulfillment of Bezos's vision. As a part of Team Amazon, he bought into the company dream and he works tirelessly to fulfill it.

In the words of Steve Jobs, "When I hire somebody really senior, competence is the ante. They have to be really smart. But the real issue for me is, are they going to fall in love with Apple? Because if they fall in love with Apple, everything else will take care of itself. They'll want to do what's best for Apple, not what's best for them, what's best for Steve, or anybody else."[5]

Steve Jobs created one of the most universally loved brands, yet he did not build the Apple name by being lovable and personally charming. In fact, he was the opposite. He has been described by many as downright cruel and narcissistic.

---

[5] Betsy Morris, "Steve Jobs Speaks Out," *Business Insider*, March 7, 2008, http://archive.fortune.com/galleries/2008/fortune/0803/gallery.jobsqna.fortune/index .html

In 2014, Ken Rosen, a former Apple and NeXT employee told *Business Insider*, "When [Jobs] was good, he was better than his reputation. When he was rough on people, he was worse than you could ever imagine."[6] But, without his dark side, he never would have aspired to believe he could change the world. His unifying vision was born from his personal sense of grandeur and was fostered by his focus on detail, minutiae, and aesthetics. He knew what he wanted and would never settle for anything less. His vision was precise, clear, and bigger than the average leader would dare to create.

Apple started out making computers. A fine and valuable task, but "making computers" was not founder Steve Jobs's unifying vision. A good thing for Apple, as it would not have been one to motivate a team to grow the company into the most profitable in the United States.[7] Even a vision of "making computers and becoming the most profitable company in the United States" wouldn't have gotten Apple to its summit.

The unifying vision Steve Jobs introduced to his team in 1980 included the statement, "To make a contribution to the world by making tools for the mind that advance humankind." Because of his relentless pursuit of a perfect implementation of his big picture, he—like Bezos—resorted to name-calling and confrontation when the people deviated from his vision. But the result was as grand as the vision itself. Not only did his team fall in love with Apple, but his customer base embraced

---

[6] *Business Insider*, http://www.businessinsider.com, Working With Steve Jobs, Summed Up by a Former apple employee, October 14, 2014

[7] 63rd Edition (June 7, 2017) Fortune 500; Apple, *Fortune* 500 Rank: No. 3, 2016 Profits: $45.7 billion % of Revenues (Margin): 21%

the brand with an obsessive loyalty that can only be described as love. Or possibly iLove. With each new Apple product release, Applephiles eagerly await the next new release date. This kind of dedication is not born from a vision that is unclear and ill-defined. It is inspired by a vision that is demanding and specific. Customers know that Apple will not let them down; They bought into the Apple ideal, and they love whatever is next, sight unseen. Because of Jobs's unwillingness to sacrifice his vision, the company lives on and grows exponentially, and his bigger-than-life vision thrives today.

Your unifying vision should make people fall in love with the company you are leading. Not everyone will fall in love with it, but you can make staff changes so that the right people can gravitate toward the opportunity to ascend as meaningful contributors.

Be Present

"Keep your attention focused on the work, be alert and ready to handle ably and intelligently any situation which may arise—this is mindfulness."
Thich Nhat Hanh, Zen Master

Be present. Being present is being mindful. Strive to be mindful in all that you do. Direct your focus to the task at hand. Presence demands that when you are doing one thing, you should only be thinking about the thing you're doing. Nothing else.

Do the one thing and focus. Do not think of things that happened earlier in the day. Do not think about your meeting yesterday. Disregard the horrible traffic that you were stuck in on your way to work. Keep your mind focused on that very moment. If you are talking to an employee, talk to that employee. If you are negotiating a transaction, be in the transaction. Make sure that you are present and engaged. You can't "get to us" when you're checked out.

Before you share your thoughts or address anyone about your vision, take a few moments to center yourself and calm your mind.

Every major influencer I know or have read about has a ritual—an exercise that they perform before they walk into a situation that requires them to be at their best. A brief period of reflection, listening to soothing music, meditation, jumping jacks, looking in the mirror and connecting to the fire in your eyes, or maybe keeping a piece of your child's school art in your briefcase that you can take out and touch. Tony Robbins jumps on a mini-tramp. One friend of mine touches his lucky tie and breathes deep before he walks on stage. Me? I listen to Pink Floyd.

Whatever it is, make up a ritual for yourself and do it. These small tasks remind you that you are about to begin something big that requires your presence and full attention. You are about to devote all of your being to the task at hand. The mindful mindset requires you to be all systems go—with no intention of failing. Your commitment to the task must be real to you, or it will never be real to anyone else. When you have faith in the mission, it is easier for others to want to be a part of it.

Keep people engaged by speaking about the vision, acknowledging the importance of each person's role in achieving it. Be as engaged with your audience as you expect them to be engaged in your vision.

You can tell when someone is not engaged and listening. Anyone can. We have all had those moments in a restaurant when we know the waiter will mess up our order because we can see that his attention is not on us. He is distracted by another table, or a fight that occurred in the kitchen, or another server. If you believe that you're fooling anyone when you are not present, the only one you're fooling is you.

When you are fully engaged in the moment, it is easier to keep others focused too, which is impossible to do if your mind has gone astray.

About twenty-five years ago, a young salesman came to my home to sell me a water purification system. I invited him onto my porch. My wife and I sat at the picnic table, and he opened the giant binder full of pictures and charts. About ten minutes into the conversation, I realized that he was mimicking every move that I made. If I scratched my head, he scratched his head. When I shifted to the left he shifted to the left. As he told me how my future would be better with his water conditioner system, all I could think was, "He must have recently attended NLP training." I had stopped listening to him. Everything he conveyed signaled that he was not sincere. He didn't care about us, only the sale. Without warning,

I stood up, smiled, took his binder, and said, "If you can tell me the benefits of your product without reading the binder, and you can do so looking me in the eyes, I will buy your water system."

He scrambled to his feet, grabbed his binder, and said, "That is not how this works!" And he left.

Sadly, he was clueless. Whether he was sincere or not, or whether or not he actually cared, there was nothing in his presentation that made me feel connected.

And, surely, nothing made him feel connected to me. He was not present in our conversation. He was following rules prescribed by a sales trainer, and he hid behind NLP training and the details in his binder. I don't believe he even asked me if I had a water purification system already. That did not matter, because I did not matter. Only the presentation mattered.

This is the folly of a lack of presence.

While I felt bad that I had pushed him over the edge, I will always be grateful to the young man for teaching me to be real and present and never to hide behind a binder of meaningless facts and data. In my career, I have considered the binder as a metaphor for a podium, crib notes, or anything that separates me from my listener.

Encourage Others to Be Present

"Life doesn't give us purpose, we give life purpose."
The Flash

As we discussed earlier, people will have roles in your big picture. Once you have placed someone in their role, they will need to be present in that role. Do not give them cause to question the role by questioning the role yourself. If the role includes decision-making power, keep it so. You must be willing to empower people to perform within the boundaries of the role you have given them without micromanaging and interfering with their success.

Allow others to make their own decisions and let them know that their knowledge is vital to your vision. In short, you have cast the roles you need people in to fulfill your vision, now trust them to act appropriately within those roles.

If someone wants to feel appreciated and wants to know that you are confident in their abilities, empower them. Let them know that you want them to find solutions to the problems they confront. Give them the power to act decisively, and the ability to go forth and do what needs to be done in such a way that they feel confident and free in their actions.

As you are putting this person into a role, make sure that the role is one that they are competent to carry out. Some people will come to you fully able to fill a role, others must be trained to do so. If you need to provide them with education and training, then see to it education is provided. If you give people the tools to be competent, their self-confidence will rise to meet the challenges the task presents. It is that self-confidence that will give them pride and commitment to execute your vision and make it their own.

Robin, a friend of mine, cheerfully recalled working at the Rock Bottom Brewery in Denver, Colorado. When she talked about her time as a waitress there, excitement was in her voice, but it was not excitement about the job of waitressing. It was the excitement of recalling the skill of her manager. The joy she recalled was the result of the way her boss made her feel as an employee. Now a white-collar professional, Robin explained that during training, the staff was advised that they were to do whatever was necessary to make the customer happy. There were no limitations so long as the customer's satisfaction was achieved.

On one evening, a couple with their young child came into the restaurant. As Robin took their order, the child insisted that she wanted Chicken McNuggets. The parents tried to explain to her that they were not at McDonald's. As they struggled to rationalize with the child, Robin took down the parents' order and entered it into the computer. Then she left the restaurant and walked three blocks to a neighboring McDonald's where she purchased a Chicken McNugget Happy Meal and returned to the restaurant. Without missing a beat, she served the family their food along with the child's meal of choice. It was a "Happy Meal" for all.

The parents were so shocked by her actions that they insisted on speaking to the manager.

The father explained that he was the administrator of a hospital in New Jersey and that he would give his right arm if he could get his staff to serve people the way that Robin had. The gentleman made it very clear that he wanted to know what the manager had done to inspire her employees so greatly that they would perform such actions on their own initiative. The conversation between the two lasted about forty minutes. Robin never learned exactly what was said during that discussion, but I trust that empowerment and trust were discussed. *Empowerment and trust.* If you want people to be inspired to fulfill your mission, you must trust them. And you demonstrate that trust by empowering them to make decisions.

The family left Robin a big tip, and the manager handed her a fifty-dollar check as a bonus. But what stuck with Robin twenty-five years after the fact was the feeling of satisfaction she felt carrying out the vision in her unique way.

When you are willing to walk to the edge of your safety zone, look into the abyss of fear, and take a risk, opportunities abound. You will never know the true potential of your dreams unless you act upon them and allow others to unleash their potential.

In the art of influence, you will never know how much someone can contribute to your dream unless you allow that person to act on their own inspiration. Sometimes you have to sacrifice your ego and let go. Sometimes you have to just let go of some of your controls and see how people handle themselves.

If you have taken the time to let people understand their role in your ultimate vision, giving them responsibility is giving them trust. Once someone knows that you trust them, they will have more confidence in what they are doing because your trust in them will reflect positively on their psyche.

_____

When you are willing to walk to the edge of your safety zone, look into the abyss of fear, and take a risk, opportunities abound.

_____

CHAPTER 8

Freedom from Micromanagement

"A leader is best when people barely know he exists,
when his work is done, his aim fulfilled,
they will say: we did it ourselves."
Lao Tzu

You will *get to us* when people enroll in your vision and want to be a part of the difference you plan to make. When people feel that achieving nobility is an available option, the need to motivate disappears. There is no longer a need to inspire your team when the vision unifies everyone under a single purpose and a common goal. To make your goal a mutual endeavor, realize that you have to let go a little bit. You have to let your ego step aside. Understand that you chose this person for a reason. Empower them to make decisions that affect the company on a scale appropriate to their position.

Whenever you wish to get another to perform a task, you have to be willing to say, "I chose this person, so I choose to trust this person. I believe this person can live up to the responsibility."

As your mission proceeds, be sure to stay present with the vision. It's the best way to keep people invested in your goal.

When I think of the great leaders, one of the first that comes to my mind is John F. Kennedy who, during his inaugural address, said "Ask not what your country can do for you, ask what you can do for your country." Prior to speaking this now famous quote, he promised that, "The energy, the faith, the devotion which we bring to this endeavor will light our country and all who serve it, and the glow from that fire can truly light the world."

With this phrase, Kennedy introduced his unifying vision. He asked the American people to commit themselves to a better world. In that vision, he promised that those who came forward to serve would glow in the light that resulted from success. He offered an opportunity to be a part of something greater that brought people together to desire—as one—the outcome he envisioned. Later, when President Kennedy was assassinated, Jacqueline Kennedy, gave an interview in which she sought to inspire the world to remember the Kennedy Presidency as "one brief shining moment that was known as Camelot."

Her reference to the shining light in Camelot renewed the Kennedy message and gave birth to a legend by comparing her husband's Presidency to Camelot. The positive image of King Arthur's court created a myth that has fueled generations. People saw their personal ability to carry out the hope and potential offered up during Kennedy's inaugural speech as an opportunity for them to each sit at the roundtable as nobles.

Kennedy urged his generation to achieve nobility by answering his call to create an America with high standards of strength and sacrifice. Notice his message revolved around the people to whom he spoke. It did not revolve around him. Had Kennedy addressed the nation speaking of himself, the country, and what he would do, there would have been no room for anyone to feel their own opportunity for greatness. When your leadership is about the people you lead, there is room for everyone at the table. If people can see how their role makes a difference, they will become engaged, and you will not need to spend every waking hour micromanaging your teams. A vision that energizes your team makes them respond to the task at hand with enthusiasm.

Make It Personal

I believe every group of people is a living organism. And if you can speak to a group of people and make it personal to them, you can get them to understand you better. It may not always hit at the heart and soul of who they are individually, but you can move the audience as a personalized unit. For instance, if I am speaking to the assembly floor at a factory, I have to be aware of their concerns and be respectful of their work and the challenges they face.

Everyone has a task to do. Each person is doing the same thing over and over again all day long. At the Martin guitar factory, they're cutting guitar tops, they're framing, they're setting necks. They all have different jobs, but they each understand that they are not merely building a guitar, they are building a legend.

If you ever have the good fortune to go on a factory tour, your guide will be one of the factory artisans who has volunteered to leave their station on the floor to lead it. When someone who spends their day repetitively inserting metal in the neck of the guitar tells you they have a cool job, you know you've arrived at a special place. And no, she was not an anomaly.

I have toured the Martin factory more times than I care to admit, and I have never encountered anyone who lacks pride in the product they create. They are excited to meet each Martin guitar owner that tours the factory.

If you speak to the workers as you move through the line, you'll find that they are very proud to tell you what they do and what their passions are. They're all different. One looked like a middle-aged rock 'n' roll guy, one millennial showed so much interest in the wood grains and finish I wondered if at home she was also a woodworker, and a matronly woman looked like someone I'd expect to have a penchant for baking pies. They are a diverse group, but when it comes to Martin, they all care about the same thing: That they are given enough room to do their job and take pride in it. The tours are an opportunity to share their pride in what they do with customers and fans.

Chris Martin has created an environment where employees thrive because he has addressed the personal needs of those who live in Nazareth, Pennsylvania and make his guitars. Some of those people have been working there for thirty years.

Martin's unifying vision centers around exceptional leadership and innovation coming out of a traditional, family-owned company. Martin's taking his unifying vision to the ultimate means that what began in 1833 as a family business has become an *extended* family business. He has personalized the worker's experience because they have been given enough space to do their jobs in a safe environment, with a sense of family, and they're encouraged to enjoy themselves as they do something important.

The workers at Martin, just like those at Apple, and Amazon, and GM, have been provided a unifying vision that enables them to step into the light of a nobler cause than just going to work and picking up a paycheck. The idea of being a part of a team working together towards something that is bigger than any one member, including the CEO, transcends personality clash and selfish desires. This isn't a promise of no conflict or never needing to course correct or let some people go, but the more clarity and meaning you bring to your vision, the less time you will invest in micromanagement and oversight. Your ability to consistently lead with a unifying vision will get everyone you lead to "us."

Once you unite people in a vision which provides a path to nobility, nothing is beyond your reach. You can accomplish anything.

AFTERWORD:
FINAL THOUGHTS

"Success is not final, failure is not fatal:
it is the courage to continue that counts."
Winston Churchill

As you look at your goals and your team, always remember that human nature drives us all to want to be a part of something. The bigger your vision becomes, the more opportunities will exist for people to rise with you and share in the nobility that comes from their accomplishments. When you give others the opportunity to succeed, your success will be their success.

As your team grows, you become more aware of the needs of others, and you will learn more about yourself. As you learn and grow, allow the new you to revisit your vision to determine whether it can be made larger than the old you imagined; give your vision the freedom to expand beyond your imagination. Your team's ideas and ambition will become new energy to feed your unifying vision and further drive your success. Do not be afraid of the growth the vision experiences from the unified momentum.

It is my hope that the thoughts that I have shared with you will inspire you to grow into your vision so that newer, better, and bigger dreams will await you.

The information in *Getting to 'Us'* can make a profound difference in your life and career, but only if you put it to work.

To help you along your journey, I've created a quick free training: *Double Your Ability to Influence in Under 10-minutes.* Go here to check it out: www.GettingtoUsBook.com/gift

If you would like more help creating a unified vision and bringing it to your team, or if you want to share any comments, feel free to email me at Joe@TheMindShark.com.

ACKNOWLEDGMENTS

This book was born from my enjoyable career as a law firm manager, business consultant, and courtroom attorney. I am grateful for the many clients and team members with whom I have worked closely to acquire the skills of management, human understanding, and the wisdom to make this book possible.

I am thankful to my mentor and book coach, Robin Colucci. Robin remained committed to helping me clarify my thoughts. And—in spite of my stubbornness—she retrained this lawyer to write like a human. Without her support, my thoughts would have remained lost in the ether.

Thank you to Jason Liller for assisting me through the editing and publishing process. I would be remiss if I did not acknowledge Jason for the many years of friendship. Our shared mutual addiction to books fueled my desire to be an author.

Last, and certainly not least, thank you to my family. My wife, Deb, and our daughters, Olivia and Kaela, were always willing to read the first, second, and twenty-seventh drafts. They did so with love. Their support was inspiring and invaluable. Thank you.

ABOUT THE AUTHOR

JOE CURCILLO is a consultant who helps company leaders engage their teams to enthusiastically achieve any outcome they desire. After practicing law for more than thirty years and managing his own successful law firm, Joe followed his passion for helping people communicate more effectively, and applies it to deliver speeches, training, and executive coaching to enable people to become empowering leaders.

Joe Curcillo earned his JD from Temple University School of Law. During his thirty-year-long legal career, he served as an adjunct professor of law teaching advocacy by developing a hands-on course that uses the art of storytelling as a communication tool. Joe now uses the skills of advocacy, storytelling, and management to guide his clients to be more effective. His work has been published in *Speaker Magazine, Sales & Service Excellence,* and *Pennsylvania Lawyer.*

Joe is also an internationally acclaimed award-winning mentalist entertainer. Using the powers of observation and the skills that he mastered selecting thousands of jurors, Joe "reads the minds" of his audience, stretching the power of perception beyond the imagination.

He resides in Harrisburg, Pennsylvania with his wife, the Honorable Judge Deborah Curcillo, and their daughters, Olivia and Kaela, who are both aspiring young professionals.